Around

Stony Stratford

A THIRD SELECTION

St John's Ambulance competition held at the Gables, Wolverton (built 1896) home of the Carriage Superintenden L&NWR, 1897 or 1898. Clocks and tea sets were awarded to the winning team. Jonathan Knight, First Foremai of the Joiners' Shop, is in the centre of the photograph, below the top row. Mary Knight, wife of Jonathan, is in th back row of nurses, fifth from the right. Archie Knight, son of Jonathan, a Trimmer, is in the front row of men seventh from the right. Owen Knight, son of Jonathan, a Joiner, is in the back row, second from the left. Mr C.A Park, Works Superintendent, is on the left front, wearing a hard hat. Dr W.H. Bull snr, of Stony Stratford, is on th extreme right, holding his top hat and walking stick.

BRITAIN IN OLD PHOTOGRAPHS

Around *Stony Stratford*

A THIRD SELECTION

AUDREY LAMBERT

SUTTON PUBLISHING LIMITED

Sutton Publishing Limited
Phoenix Mill · Thrupp · Stroud
Gloucestershire · GL5 2BU

First published 2000

Copyright © Audrey Lambert, 2000

Half-title page photograph: Group of lacemakers, Shenley, Bucks, *c.* 1910; *title page photograph:* Wendy Tipple of Castlethorpe when she was Merry Comrades Carnival Queen at Hanslope, *c.* 1961.

British Library Cataloguing in Publication Data
A catalogue record for this book is available from the British Library.

ISBN 0-7509-2366-0

Typeset in 10.5/13.5 Photina.
Typesetting and origination by
Sutton Publishing Limited.
Printed and bound in England by
J.H. Haynes & Co Ltd, Sparkford.

A full stocklist of over 700 titles in this series is available from
Toby Waller, Sutton Publishing, Phoenix Mill, Thrupp, Stroud, Gloucestershire, GL5 2BU.

The Railway Queen visits Wolverton, *c.* 1953–4. The competition was open throughout the railway system and the winner went once during the year to all railway towns. The photograph was taken outside the Works Canteen. Back row, extreme left: Fireman Fred Ratcliffe; extreme right: Fireman Vic Sapwell. These two were actual firemen from the Works Fire Brigade. Front row, left to right: Pat Osborne, the Railway Queen, Bessie Smart, Beryl Green.

Contents

Mr David Jones, Headmaster, with pupils in Group No. 1 (there were several groups of different pupil photographed at this time) outside the British School, corner of High Street and Wolverton Road, Stony Stratford *c.* 1898. The school was built in 1844 by subscription at a cost of about £800. There was a public room over it fo the use of the town generally. This school catered for both boys and girls who did not attend the Church c England Schools – St Giles' (boys) and St Mary's (girls and infants). The school closed in 1907 when the nev Council School opened in Russell Street. Back row, left to right: -?-, -?-, -?-, Alfred George Cooper, brother to secon row eighth from left, -?-, Bert Mackerness. Second row: David Jones, with hands on Alice Clark, Christine ?, Florri Fancutt, Wilfred Bridgman, Ellis Hillier, Arthur Hillier, brother to back row third from right, Emily Mackerness Florrie Meakins, Pupil Teacher. Third row: Grace Mackerness, -?-, -?-, Alf Mackerness, ? Meakins, -?-, Anni Holman, Ada Hillier, -?-, Elsie Hillier. Front row: -?-, -?-, -?-, ? Holman, Willie Mackerness, Sidney Mackerness, -?- ? Meakins.

INTRODUCTION

Welcome to the third compilation of 'Photographs Around Stony Stratford'. I am sure you will find this edition easily as fascinating, if not more so, than those published previously.

I have known the author, Audrey Lambert, since we were both fourteen years old, when we joined the Stony Stratford Ranger Company under its captain Miss Effie Pillow. We were soon asked to help with 2nd Stony Stratford Cub Pack, led by Mrs Campbell and from that time met many of the people who are featured in this book.

Audrey has, of course, met many others over recent years who have helped her in her unremitting detective work, remembering and recording people and occasions of Stony Stratford's past and the local area, and has, despite the exigencies of her meticulous research, enjoyed the task and made many new friends.

As an 'old' friend, Audrey has kept me in touch with the life of the district over the years since our early days, when we explored many of the places mentioned in this book, and I have very happy memories of those days. I wish her, her husband Jim and all those who have contributed to this historical account every success and happiness in this millennium. Thanks must go to the many, many people, too numerous to be identified here, who have made this such a nostalgic experience.

Joy M. Brunt (née Small)
formerly of 62 London Road,
Stony Stratford
100th Mayor of Swindon, Wilts 1999/2000

On a cold winter's day, perhaps February or March, a group of fans wait for a football match to commence i Wolverton Park, *c.* 1945–6. The photograph was taken by the bottom goal posts near the gas works. The railwa station railings, behind which the trains pass, can be seen in the background. The group includes Billy Dew, Erni Sprittles, Dolly Cunniffe, Len Bellamy, Hubert Skinner, Bert Clarke, Bill Webb, Archie Godwin, Bill Cornhill, Oll Johnson, George Jones, Dorothy Snowdon, Sam Iles, Mr Clark snr, Lewis Clark (son of Mr Clark), Bill Jakeman sn Bill Jakeman jnr, Mary Jakeman, Johnny Humphries, Mr Lucas snr and Dennis Lucas (son of Mr Lucas).

1

My Town – Stony Stratford

Volverton Town Band turning from Coronation Road into London Road, *c.* 1960. Reg Barden, in the second rank n the left, is playing the double bass, while one of the tall Dytham brothers is playing the trombone in the front f the picture.

The crowning of Stony Stratford's first Carnival Queen outside the police station in the Market Square at the hospital fête, 1935. Colonel L.C. Hawkins is introducing Mrs P.Y. Atkinson of Cosgrove to crown the Carnival Queen. Left to right: Eileen Young, Irene Clarke, Irene (Rene) Butler (Carnival Queen), Olive French, Maud Wildman. At the front are pages Geoffrey Waymark and Bernard Young. (Photograph by Fred G. Bavey)

Members of the Ancell Trust Tennis Club on a float at the Carnival, *c.* 1935. Commemorating twenty-five years between 1910 and 1935, those standing are dressed as players from years ago while those at the front are seen in the current tennis wear. All were unmarried at the time, but eventually: back row, left to right: Louie Fountaine married Dick Saunders, Basil Stanton married Linda Wilmin. Front row: Harry Wells married Edna Fancutt, Irene Stanton married Allen Holland.

Ian Phelps playing cricket, with big brother Ron as wicket-keeper in the field at the rear of their home, 119 High Street, *c.* 1933–4. Their father, Wilkie J. Phelps, was a baker and confectioner there. In the background is the famous horse 'Blackie' who, on the bread round, set off at the 'click-click' signal, and knew all the stopping places en route – probably more clever than delivery boys!

A scene from *The Sound of Music*, the first production that the New City Players presented at Wolverton College of Further Education, 1974. The cast included approximately forty people. Back row, left to right: Peter Folwell, David Whitlock, Ian Warner. Centre row: June Thorpe, Syd Pearson. Front row: Michael Folwell. Their producer, Joan Walker, some twenty-five years and seventy productions later, now has three productions each year, covering a variety of musicals, pantomimes and plays. More recently a concert has been added to the Players' repertoire.

Enjoying a ride in the boat in the Recreation Ground, 1938. Left: Joyce Mander; centre: Ruth Peet, right: Doreen Mander. Ruth's mother, Mrs Martha Peet, looks on. In the background is the very popular slide.

'Yorky' (Bill Williamson) with his grinding machine on his bicycle on which he sharpened knives, scissors, etc. Arriving in the area in about 1948, he called each week at the food shops in the High Street, collecting scraps of bacon, cheese and stale loaves, enough to last a week, which he supplemented with rabbits and vegetables. He ended his days in a hovel at Cattle Ford Bridge on the Buckingham Road, and is buried in Thornton churchyard.

Stony Stratford Red Cross in the Senior School, 1960–1. The instructors were Miss Zillah Full and Nurse Mary Tanner. Back row, left to right: Jane Tyrrell, Margaret Pratt, Rosemarie Bird, Pam Nicholls, -?-, -?-, Cynthia Dickinson, Patsy Richardson, -?-. Front row: -?-, Carol Canvin, Mary Kenny, Linda Langdon, -?-, Ann Read, Susan Roberts, Frances Walker.

Stony Stratford Army Cadet Corps, photographed during the Second World War, *c.* 1944. Camps were held near to Soulbury and at Penn Wood, near High Wycombe. Formed in 1943–4, they were Message Runners for the Home Guard. Back row, left to right: -?-, Geoff Beer, Reg Wright, Peter Collins. Centre Row: Bill Dunckley, Ray Phillips, Lt. Col. Donald Campbell, Ken MacPhearson, Stan Richardson. Front row: Tony King, Ken Tandy.

Samuel Holland and family, *c.* 1912. He built the family home, 2 Vicarage Road, and the row of cottages nearby. His business included market gardening, farming, selling coal, furniture storage and removals. Back row, left to right: Walter (blacksmith, George Yard, Stony Stratford), Kate Rebecca, Amy Jane, Jessie (married Ernest Wickens, 82 High Street, draper, ladies' and gents' shoes etc. and 59 High Street, furniture), Elizabeth (married Harry Dewick, painter and decorator. A son, Leonard, had an electrical shop at 40 and 38 High Street), Herbert Cecil (married Jinny, a daughter of Mills, the florist in Market Square). Front row: Stafford (in family business, married Eva Cattell), Samuel Holland (came from Totternhoe, Bedfordshire, in 1872, married Jane Johnson of Towcester), George Henry (farmer, married Edith Grace Betts).

St Giles', Stony Stratford, bellringers' outing, 14 August 1954. This was organised by Bert Edwards, Tower Captai of St Giles', and the photograph was taken in Fairford, Gloucestershire. The group includes: Jim Lambert, Joh Eales, Reg Hall, Mrs Billy French, Billy Dillow, Reg Howson, Mrs Edwards, Mrs Yates, John Higgins, Tom Trasler Jack Chance, Bill Clark, Ted Lambert, Mrs Bill Clark, Mrs Durrant, Bert Edwards, Tommy Roberts, George Atkins Bob Abrahams, Freddie Case, John Dillow, Bill French, Mr Valentine, Mrs Hilda Valentine, Mrs Billy Dillow Graham Yates, Edie Daniels, Mrs Chance and Edwin 'father' Yates. (Photograph by Bert (Algie) Daniels)

A group of bellringers from the Oxford Guild, North Bucks Branch, at a ringing meeting and tea at Newton Longville, mid-1950s. Back of tables, right to left: Gillian Shaw, Malcolm Hooton, Vic Adams, Arthur Armstrong, Mrs Wright (wife of Canon Kenneth Wright), Denny Hurst, Bill Yates, Kay Yates, George Holland, -?-. Front of tables, right to left: -?-, Billy French, Jim Lambert, Bert Edwards, Eva Edwards, Johnny Brooks, Canon Elliott Wigg, Freddie Case. (Photograph by Cecil Checkley)

Young bellringers at St Giles' Church, *c.* 1964. Clockwise, from bottom left: David Coxhill, Graham Brown, Andrew Fincher, Maureen Eglesfield, Keith Brown, Andrew Haseldine, Richard Haseldine.

The four Randall Starlets from the Gwendolyn Randall Dancing Troupe, *c.* 1945. Left to right: Margaret Goodman, Jean Seabury, Josie Scragg, Jean Bush. Margaret Goodman became one of the famous Tiller Girls.

A group of children who had been in a play produced by Beaty and Winnie Downing from the Baptist Church *c.* 1933. They are pictured on a float in a parade round the town. Back row, left to right: fairies: Phyllis Barker Betty Tooley, Joan Wain, -?-. Centre row: Bess Fensom, Emily 'Bubbles' Aries. Front row: rabbits: Dorothy Johnson -?-, Winnie Beckett, Beryl Green, Peggy Worker, Audrey Benbow.

The residents of Clarence Road enjoying a tug-o'-war contest when celebrating the Coronation of Queen Elizabeth II, 2 June 1953. John Thomas Shean (no. 51) and Mrs Edith Buxton (no. 49) stand in their doorways. Those identified on the far side, from left to right, are Jack Goodridge, Claude Bailey, David Osborne, Ken Shean, Bert Bennett, Brian Tompkins, Ken Brewer, John Osborne, David Eglesfield, Noel Eglesfield and, back right, Mr Kingston and John Aylott. Front row, second left: David Townsend. Small boy at the front on the right: Robert Valentine.

During her visit to Stony Stratford on 5 April 1966, HM Queen Elizabeth II received a bouquet from Margaret Cornford, the nine-year-old daughter of Councillor Fred Cornford, Chairman of the Wolverton Urban District Council, which then had its offices to the left of the photograph. Left: Bill Coxhill, Scout District Commissioner. Back, left to right: Charlie Saggers (Old Contemptibles), Mr Scarman (with walking stick, behind Margaret), the Revd C.L.G. Hutchings, Vicar of St Giles'. Right: Mrs Cornford, Councillor F.W. Cornford, HRH the Duke of Edinburgh.

The Stony Stratford Minors beat Newport Pagnell Minors in the final of the North Bucks League, held in Wolverton Park on Easter Saturday, 1943. Mr S. Coles, the League Chairman, presented the shield and cup to Stony Stratford who had, this season, brought off the double event, being winners of the North Bucks Minor League and North Bucks Shield. Back row, left to right: Cliff Brandom, Fred French, Bill Clarke, Ken Cleaver, Alec Levitt. Centre row: Dickie Phillips, Basil Read, Bill Daniell. Front row: Les Parker, Albert Kightley, Bob Gregory, Reg Russell (Captain), Pete Hillyer.

Stony Stratford Town Football Club was founded in 1898. This team won the North Bucks and District Shield and the Stantonbury Charity Cup in 1957. Standing, left to right: Stan Richardson, Bill Dillow, Alec Levitt, Graham Holdon, Peter Levitt, Peter Haynes, Bill Shepherd, Ken Ward, Ted Hellenburgh. Kneeling/sitting: Ron Holbrook, Peter Styles, John Dillow (with shield), Alan Bowdler, David Larner, Syd Sharp.

Rodney Cleaver marking out the wicket at Stony Stratford Sports Ground ready for the next cricket match, 1960.

Mrs Ada Wildman (left) and Mrs Clara Sibthorpe (right), members of the Stony Stratford Ladies Bowls Club, which had been formed in the 1940s. Their Bowls Green was on what is now the tennis courts in the Ancell Trust Grounds. Mrs Annie Knight was the Ladies Buckinghamshire County President, as was Mrs West. Adele, the granddaughter of another member, Mrs Marie Johnson, is carrying on the family tradition, and has played in the All-England Under 25s. The club temporarily disbanded, but reformed in 1978, and now has almost forty members. In early days salad teas were produced for visiting teams in their primitive kitchen. Today, with fitted kitchen, they produce sumptuous meals and are renowned for their trifles when hosting a county game.

Stony Stratford Rugby Football Club, 1935/6. The club played 21 games, won 11, lost 9 and drew 1. Total points: for: 160, against: 151. The winners of the Northampton Seven-a-Side Tournament are seen here. Back row, left to right: M. Whiting, G. Weston, R. Wills, J. Hewitt, R. Wylie. Middle row: P. Edwards (groundsman), R. Dickens, D. Roberson, R. Caesar, C. Spickernell, A. Bowden, L. Roberson, C. Neale, Capt. E. Chambers (referee). Front row: E. Adams, D. Wood, J. Roberson (vice-captain), A. Wood (captain), C.H. Weston Esq. (chairman), J. Weston, R. Elliott.

Walter Franklin (centre) and two friends who were all keen cyclists, 1930s. They wore plus-fours (which had been first used by golfers) so they didn't need to wear cycle clips. Walter was a member of the WAAC which was formed at about the same time as the opening of Wolverton Park in 1885.

Sunday School teachers at St Mary's Church setting off for an outing to Haversham (4 miles away!), *c.* 1912. Standing, left to right: the Revd A.J. Moxon, -?-, -?-, -?-, Harold Phillips. Seated: Mrs Hugh Williams, -?-, Florence Cooper, Ted Beard (killed in the First World War), -?-.

The Centenary Dedication Festival of St Mary the Virgin Church was held on Sunday 29 September 1963. It was attended by Mrs H.J. Carpenter in five capacities: as the granddaughter of the founder of St Mary's Church, the Revd W.P. Trevelyan, who was Vicar of Old Wolverton (1856–71) and Rector of Calverton (1859–81); as her father was the Revd G.P. Trevelyan, Vicar of St Mary's (1885–97); as wife of the Lord Bishop; as Diocesan President of the Mother's Union; and on this occasion as chauffeur to the Bishop! The photograph was taken at the Agape the previous evening. Left to right: Lesley Cooper (churchwarden), the Revd C.L.G. Hutchings (St Giles'), Mrs Carpenter, the Revd H. Francome Painter (St Mary's), the Lord Bishop of Oxford, Mrs Painter, Mr W. Dillow (churchwarden).

Wolverton St Mary's Infant School, 1899. Back row, left to right: Miss Nessie Keveren (teacher), Albert Percy, ? Brown, Florence Amelia Cooper, ? Brown, Willie Holton, Tom Downing, Willie Saunders, Miss Ethel Ward (teacher). Second row: -?-, Fanny Wright, Laura Neal, Nellie Clark, Edith Speaks, E. Green, ? Green, Winnie Oak, Gertie Kimble. Third row: -?-, Jessie Smith, -?-, Elsie Britten, Annie Biddle, Ethel Smith, T. Smith, Ernie Pratt, ? Lankester. Front row: -?-, Ted Stevens, Tom Swain, Tom Jolley, -?-, Willie Claydon.

St Mary's School, *c.* 1925. Back row, left to right: third: Florence (Flo) Johnson, sixth: Edna Goodridge, seventh: Amy Tucker, eighth: Miss Ada Plumb (teacher). Front row, second from the left: Evelyn Read.

Russell Street Infants' School, 1956. Back row, left to right: Ron Baker, -?-, Monty Lynds, Robert Adams, Tom Underhill. Second row: Conrad Winchcombe, Michael Stewart, -?-, George Gauluska, Clive Burgess, Michael Brassett, Michael Fleming, Ian Alderman, Edward Watts, Barry Wilkinson, C. Kirkman. Third row: ? Panter, Julie Evans, Julie Gilles, Jill and Jennifer Valentine (twins), Valerie Spencer, Pam Nicholls, Stefanie French, Rosemarie Bird, Jane Gubrick, Christine Stanton, Diane Harris, Miss Morris (teacher). Front row: Sue Roberts, -?-, Susan Holland, Marion Doyle, Pam Sibthorpe, Linda Langdon, Carol Canvin, Lyn Baines, -?-, -?-, Maureen Langley, Ann Read.

St Giles' Church of England Boys' School, Standards 4, 5, 6 and 7, *c*. 1926. Back row, left to right: Bill Page, Francis Dewick, Les Nicholls, Tom White, W.J. Toms (Headmaster). Second row: Albert Bazeley, Ted Waine, Thomas Hyde, -?-, Len Sharpe, Hubert Grace, Alan Blair, Stan Robinson, Sid Savage, ? Read, Len Grace, George Webb, Stan Tucker, Stan Lovesy. Third row: Jack Nicholls, Danny Roberts, Bert Savage, Hugh Johnson, George Dicks, Bill Capel, Bob Caudle, Les Sabins, Fred Eaton, Oliver Johnson, Owen Fensom, Tim Bramley, Sid Levitt, Jack Frost, -?-. Fourth row: Harold Clarke, -?-, Allen Holland, Bert Tucker, Bernard Daniels, Bill James, ? Sabin, Bill Johnson, Ted Church, Ken Sawford, Francis Green, Claude Bailey, -?-, Sam Abbott. Front row: Jack Cohen, Ted Daniels, Charlie Whitehead, Fred Levitt, Frank Coles, John Blair, Eric Stevens, Bill Goodridge, George Shurmer, Danny Bourne, Charlie Gould, Joe Pritchett, Lesley Savage, Bert Freer (also known by the name Meakins) a Belgian boy, Ted Leonard.

St Giles' Church of England Boys' School, woodwork room, *c*. 1928. Back row, left to right: -?-, -?-, Eddie or Nelson Grace, teacher not known. Front row: -?-, -?-, -?-, George Shurmer, Tom Clarke.

Stony Stratford Primary School football team, 1970. The photograph was taken from just inside the school grounds in Vicarage Walk at the Recreation Ground end. The chimney-pots belong to the last house in Vicarage Walk; the nearer building is in the school grounds. The master is Mr A.N. Allen. Back row, left to right: Gregory Brown, Kevin Green, Michael Bull, Graham Sharp, Ian Sherwood, Kevin Shouler, Stephen Taylor. Second row: Kevin Griffiths, Richard Bird, Joey Grey (with ball), Robert Bird, David West. Front row: Andrew Durkin, Julian Rose.

Russell Street School staff – Nursery and Primary School, *c.* 1973. Back row, left to right: Gladys Cropper (Nursery School), Barbara Sandwith, Jo ?, Lesley Moore, Olive Dewhurst, Sheila Ervine, Brenda Starling, Evelyn Bold, Sheila Merry, Pauline Wheeler. Front row: Jill Gocher, Rosie Pichowski, Sadie Rothwell, Tom Lynam (caretaker), Margaret Chapman, Joan Smith (school secretary), Joan Whetstone, Stephanie Devenish, Janine Lal.

Dedication of St Giles' and St Mary's Church of England School, 24 July 1937. Back, left to right: the Revd E.J. Payne MA, Vicar of Wolverton St Mary, the Revd E.A. Steer MA, Vicar of Stony Stratford. Front: the Bishop of Buckingham, who dedicated the new school, Lord Cottesloe CB, Lord Lieutenant of Bucks. The tablet unveiled by Lord Cottesloe, recording how and when the school was built, was the gift of Mr Smith, the architect.

St Mary and St Giles' School Girls' Choir, *c.* 1953. Back row, left to right: Susan Thornton, -?-, Brenda Swann, Diana Haycock, Edna Davey, Ann Underhill, -?-, ? Frisby, Alva Westley, -?-. Second row: Pat Brown, Christine Ley, Beatrice Betts, Jennifer Smith, Maureen Griffiths, Pam Smith, Ann Barley, Barbara Dickens, Jean Dearn, Doreen Russell. Third row: Elizabeth Richardson, Janet Benn, Ann Chipperfield, Rosemary Rodwell, Ann Hepworth, Delia Mackerness, Barbara Hind, Yvonne Mackerness, Ann Fisher, Caroline Nicholls, Mr W. Rayner (teacher). Front row: Pam Roff, Janet Scott, Rosemary Inns, Denise Duggan, Maureen Smith, Pam Walker, Hazel Wilkes, Janet Skipper, Ann Underwood.

St Mary and St Giles' Senior School, *c.* 1957. Back row, left to right: Douglas Freeman, Terry Adams. Middle row: Hayden Shirley, Leslie Wootton, Roger Dunckley, Gordon Griffiths, Peter Ratcliffe, John Franklin, Nicky Verall, John Smythe, Michael Webb, Arthur Bluck. Front row: Ann Barby, Margaret Ley, Mary Richardson, Mrs Noreen Llewellyn (teacher), Linda Pettifer, Margaret Haysted, Edna Yallop, Lorraine Smith.

York House School: a class is assembled outside the French windows, 1937. Pupil Connie Rix is standing talking with the teacher, Miss Viccars. The author, Audrey Lambert (née Waine), is seen with a long pigtail down her back. The small tree in the foreground had green pods hanging on it in the summer. The pupils, having been forbidden to touch them, often dared each other to pinch one: they went off with a loud pop!

Wesley's Elm Tree in the Market Square in its prime, *c.* 1910. Within the last few years vandals have set fire to it twice and it has barely survived. A plaque by the tree records: 'John Wesley visited Stony Stratford five times and it's reputed that at least once he stood beneath this tree and preached.'

A group of pupils from York House School, *c.* 1932. Back row, left to right: Barbara Turney, Maudie Valentine, Peggy Biddis, Marjorie Dumbleton, Joan Gardner. Middle row: Yvonne Leigh, Leslie White, Miss Clarke (teacher), Philip Whiting, Roland Bennett. Front row: ? Price, Margaret Henson.

Stony Stratford Land Rangers' stall at Northampton hospital fête, June 1934. Left to right: -?-, Rene Dix, Daisy Haynes, Evelyn 'Dimp' Ware.

Ooh! That smells good! Guides from York House School Company (formed in 1920) cook their supper, on a summer evening in Turney's Field, Old Wolverton, 1935. (This is now a balancing lake for Milton Keynes.) The Guide leader was Miss Bodsworth. Left to right: Irene Andrews, Helen Campbell, -?-, Margaret Henson, Beryl Walters, Doris Wilson, Betty Dyke, Betty Clamp.

At the Royal Show, local Guiders show off their Wolverton District county banner, 3 July 1972. Note the swan, the county emblem for Buckinghamshire, and their motto '*ad astra*' (to the stars). Back row: left to right: -?-, Enid Meacham, Ivy Patterson, -?-, -?-, Dot Munday, Edie Canvin, -?-, -?-, Rose Barden, -?-. Front row: Nellie Negus, Nellie Dillow.

Friends of Guiding mending the Wolverton District county banner, *c.* 1990. Clockwise from front left: Mary Webb (née Jackson), Rene Healey (née West), Lena Jakeman, Betty West (née Kightley). The banner was designed by Mrs Enid Meacham (née Walton), and each Guide and Guider in the district worked a stitch. The banner was paraded at the first county banner service in 1928 and is one of the last remaining original banners.

1st Stony Stratford Scouts gym display team, *c.* 1919. The team was in much demand for a number of years a fêtes and other fund-raising events throughout the area. This shows one of the six different finales they coul provide to end their display. Holding hands, left to right: A Bonham, S. Gammage, G. Roberts, C. Hollyoake W. Harris, A. Giles, S. Nicholls, W. Flint. In white: H. Bennett. Centre group: E. Kirk (kneeling), A. Jackso (standing). On platform: F. Simkins (kneeling), A. Church and E. Lines holding W. Brown (centre), R. Co (kneeling), M. Coe (standing), ? Chapman (kneeling). Sitting under platform: H. Saunders and E. Rice.

Mrs Ruby Fisher who celebrated her hundredth birthday on 18 January 2000, is seen here when, as Ruby Birkby from Yorkshire, she joined the Women's Land Army in the First World War; it was formed in 1917 and this photograph dates from about 1919. Ruby worked with horses on an estate in Lincolnshire. 'Jolly' was her favourite horse. In the fields some jobs were teddering (dragging straw or hay into straight lines) and using an Oxford 'Rimroll' to break up clods of earth. She did not have to do 'fettling' (a Yorkshire expression for feeding horses at night) as a man was employed to do it.

The wedding of Herbert Waine of Launton, Oxfordshire, and Florence Amelia Cooper at St Mary's Church, 29 March 1921. Pillowlace made by the bride's grandmother, Elizabeth Willett of Shenley, can be seen edging her dress. The bridegroom has a buttonhole of lilies of the valley. The two bridesmaids, Nancy Williams (left, a music pupil of the bride) and Louisa Waine (the bridegroom's niece), both wore blue crêpe de chine dresses with a wide blue ribbon tied at the back, and straw hats with artificial flowers. Their petticoats and knickers were edged with pillowlace, and they wore white cotton stockings and white shoes. All three dresses were made by the bride. The cake, from Lever Bros, 63 Wolverton Road, weighed 21 lbs and cost £3 3*s*.

London and North Western Railway dray outside St Mary's School (now the Plough Inn), *c.* 1910. Goods that had been transported by rail to Wolverton station were delivered by this means around the area at least until the Second World War. Livestock (for example boxes of day-old chicks) had to be delivered within twenty-four hours of dispatch.

Peter Phillpotts in a shadowgraph photo by his father, Percy Phillpotts, *c.* 1926. Peter followed his father as owner/pharmacist of Cox & Robinson Ltd, 75 High Street, now the Stratford Arcade.

Edwin (Ted) Clarke with his young brother Jim, who has a mass of blonde curls and is wearing a dress, as was the fashion for small boys prior to starting school. Edwin has a mourning band on his jacket sleeve, perhaps for the death of King Edward VII in 1910 or for a member of his family, as these, or black diamonds, were regularly worn for a six-month period of mourning.

Queens Oak Border Morris was formed in about 1984 and takes its name from the tree in Potterspury under which Edward IV is said to have met Lady Elizabeth Grey, formerly Elizabeth Woodville of Grafton Regis. The side dance the Border tradition, which is found mainly in the Hereford and Shropshire region. They are seen here dancing at Stoke Bruerne locks in about 1990. At the front on the left is Sue Vinden, the owner of the photograph. The beginning of the 'folk revival' dates from Boxing Day 1899, when Cecil Sharp first saw and recorded the Morris at Headington, near Oxford.

Pillowlace pupils of Mrs Dora Clark (née Mackerness) at the third Newport Pagnell Lace Day, Ousedale School, Saturday 15 November 1980. Left to right: Ruth Atkins, Dora Clark, Audrey Cooper, Rose Holes (from Hanslope), Joan Mapley (from Hanslope).

A group of friends enjoying the sport of go-kart racing, late 1960s. This go-kart was purchased second-hand, a vintage 200cc engine was installed and it was entered in Class 4. They raced at many places including Kimbolton and Silverstone. In no. 14 is Peter Roberts and behind him are Roy Green (left) and Roger Dunckley (right). (Photograph taken by David Wise)

Two popular comedians, brothers Reg Russell (a 'Chelsea Pensioner') and Stan (his 'wife'). From 1970 to 1980 they entertained at every Bowls Club and British Legion dinner, and also Christmas parties. In 1982 they appeared on the Mr and Mrs Show at Floral Hall, Southport, with Derek Batey. At Carlisle TV studios they appeared live on TV, winning the clock, tray and anniversary silver plate. In 1992 Stan entered Milton Keynes Senior Citizen Talent Competition, borrowing a police helmet from Wolverton police station and winning the contest with his performance of 'The Laughing Policeman'. He also won in 1993, and represented Milton Keynes in the area final in Crawley with a comedy song. In 1994 he dressed as a schoolboy and sang 'Grandad' on Anglia TV.

'he presentation in Stony
Stratford Conservative Club of two
neerschaum pipes to Sir Frank
Markham, who was, as the
etiring MP, retiring as President
f the club. He had been MP for
hirteen years. At the General
lection on Thursday
28 February 1974 Bill Benyon
vas elected MP for the North
Bucks constituency, and was
onsequently the new President.
ir Frank, who was born in Stony
tratford, was knighted in 1953.
eft to right: Clarence 'Spike'
Dolling (Secretary, Conservative
Club), Elizabeth Benyon, Sir Frank
Markham, Bill Benyon, Lady
Markham, Archie Chapman
Chairman, Conservative Club).

ony Stratford Chamber of Commerce Fourth Annual Dinner at the Cock Hotel, 25 February 1960. The President as D.A. Wood, the Chairman was L.G.D. Burnham. Top table (left-hand side): Dr E. Witheridge, Jack Burnham, rs Burnham, Donald Morgan, Mrs Morgan, David Wood, Mary Wood, Harry Winsor, Doreen Winsor, Brian rnes, Mrs Barnes, Jimmy Read, Mrs Read, Len Dewick, Mrs Dewick. Front table, left to right: Alfred Cosford, orothy Chipperfield, Denis Chipperfield. Second table: Vera Sharp, Ken Sharp (Deputy Surveyor WUDC), and wife, artin Gunstone, David Yates. Third table: R.J. and Mrs Fleming, Mr and Mrs Underhill, Mr and Mrs Read. Fourth ble: Audrey and Stan Beardmore, Mr and Mrs Brookes.

Mill Drive, Stony Stratford, *c.* 1910. Older residents will remember this as a pleasant walk almost all the year round, right up to the 1950s, prior to industrial units occupying the mill and the cottage on the left, inhabited by the Oxby family, becoming derelict.

A nice view of Stratford Mill, on the left, with the Mill House and Mill Cottage, 1960s. The mill leat is running on the right of the photograph. The mill was not restored after a disastrous fire and was sadly demolished in about 1988.

Boating down the River Ouse at the bottom of the garden of Calverton House on a sunny afternoon in the 1920s. Mrs G.W. Bull is on the left, with Rita in the centre, and the Misses Maguire.

On the left is James Rogers from Stony Stratford Mill haymaking in his Mill Field with the help of Belgian First World War refugees, 1915.

This celebration dinner was held in the Scout Hall to celebrate the victory of Fred Yates as councillor in the Stony Stratford ward, Wolverton Urban District Council, for the Labour Party, May 1950. Top table, left to right: Aileen Button, Ray Bellchambers, Donald Morgan, Fred Yates, Hepzibah Yates, Alma Jacks, -?-, Dick Ellis, -?-, Mr Richardson from George Yard. The two men on the extreme right are unidentified. Nearside table, facing camera: -?-, -?-, Frank Atter, Jean Atter, Mrs Wyatt, Peter Wyatt.

Phyllis Lovesy, Stony Stratford's first Court Usher, *c.* 1978. She wore a gown over her dress and was not allowed to wear trousers. Based at Stony Stratford Court, she also deputised at Newport Pagnell and Fenny Stratford Courts. Before hearings commenced, she had to check those present, including witnesses. Phyllis would take child witnesses into the courtroom, which was upstairs, and explain the procedure. Sitting at the back, when each person was summoned she had to call them into court. She normally only worked on Fridays, the day the Stony Stratford Main Open Court was held and when the general public could sit on the back bench.

Mrs Kate Wise preparing some of her delicious dishes as cook at the Cock Hotel, here seen with the head waiter, 1955.

The girls from Wickens, drapers, 82 High Street, before the Second World War. They had to purchase material and make their own dresses; nothing was provided by the shop! Emily Kimble was in charge and always chose blue for sales assistants. Back row, left to right: Flora Ince (she worked in the office, wore navy and made her own dress), Joan Savage. Front row: Dora Bazeley (she made her own dress from a different pattern), Emily Kimble, Olive Bailey.

A play performed at Stony Stratford Methodist Church, Silver Street, early 1930s. Standing in the back row, left: Nellie Stokes. Back row, left to right: Rose Harris, Eileen Gable, Ruth Wright, Win Henson, Kathleen Parker, Jeffrey Wilson, Reg Atkins, Mrs Brown from The Gardens. Middle row: George Wilson, Norman Cosford, Joyce Cosford, Edna Richardson, Iris Brown, Eric 'Ace' Atkins, Ted Wyatt. Seated at front: Lesley Phillips, Ethel Henson, Jack Wilson, Cecil Stairs.

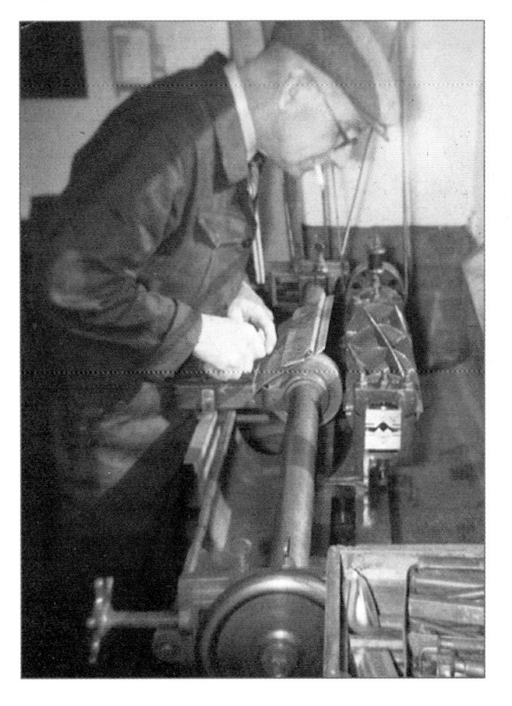

William (Bill) Jenkins was the lawnmower grinder at N.E. Chipperfield Ltd, tool dealers, hardware etc., 35–9 High Street, from 1950 to 1970.

British Legion Memorial Service, Stony Stratford, 24 June 1934. Arthur Tite, centre, wearing white gauntlet gloves, is carrying the banner for the British Legion. The parade is just passing 15 and 14 Horsefair Green on the right with the Royal Oak public house, the white building in the distance: this has since closed.

Time to put his feet up! Brian Barnes looks forward to his retirement from the family restaurant on Christmas Eve 1987. His family came from Rushden, Northamptonshire, and his father opened the Barnes Restaurant on 17 January 1937 at 117 High Street. Being situated on the busy Watling Street with much through traffic, the restaurant provided a service for travellers and visitors to the town. Brian assisted in the restaurant all his life, eventually becoming the proprietor. It closed, upon his retirement, after fifty years, and is now the Peking Restaurant.

A group of happy boys from Fegan's Homes, 1930s. They are enjoying a swim in the River Ouse from the Barley Mow bathing place, behind the paddock of the public house of that name; it is now a private residence.

One of Fegan's Homes' most adventurous 'lads', Tom McClean, in his boat *Super Silver* in which he rowed across the Atlantic alone in 1969 in the record time of seventy days. He sailed from St John's, Newfoundland on 17 May and arrived at Blacksod Bay, Co. Mayo, on 27 July. The boat is now in the Exeter Maritime Museum. He crossed the Atlantic again in *Giltspur*, only 9 ft 9 in long, leaving St John's on Tuesday 22 June 1982 and arriving fifty days later at Falmouth on Thursday 12 August.

2

Memories of a Rural Area

Peter Scarsbrook feeling adventurous as he rides his new pedal-car near his home in Hanslope, 1950s.

Repairing the roof of Hanslope Church, October 1904. A hundred years previously, on 30 June 1804, the *Northampton Mercury* reported: 'On Sunday Evening, at eight o'clock a dreadful clap of thunder, equal to the discharge of a mortar followed by most awful lightning. During the storm the lofty spire of Hanslope church was struck with lightning and almost totally destroyed. It fell with a tremendous crash and a large portion of it being precipitated upon the body of the church, part of the roof sunk along with it, the whole presenting a scene truly awful and terrific.' Originally 206 ft high, the spire when rebuilt was reduced by 20 ft.

The infants' class, Hanslope Church End School, *c.* 1920. Back row, left to right: Albert Garratt, Bert Elliot, Henry Elliot, Eric Ditum. Second row: George Keech, Ray Scarsbrook, Bill Kingston, Jack Gregory, Ted Bonner, Les Walker. Third row: Gladys Walker, Mary Sawbridge, Violet Keech, Eileen Garratt, Florrie Herbert, Florrie Herbert's younger sister, Maggie Keeves. Front row: Alfie Keeves, Tom Branson.

Wedding of two Hanslope families, 1903. Back row, second from left: Oliver Herbert. Standing in the centre, fifth from left: Tommy Herbert, who refused to wear collar and tie for this wedding of his daughter and insisted on wearing his cap! He worked on steam ploughs for Whitings and grew corn on his allotment – grist to the mill. His wife reared pigs on waste and swill. Seated in the centre, left to right: Hannah, née Howe, who first married Mr Harris and second Tommy Herbert (always an 'H'); Emma Herbert; Matilda Jane 'Tilly' Herbert, the bride, who lived to the age of ninety-six; the bridegroom Ralph Chandler, who had a smallholding in Hanslope, below the Globe Inn on Higham Cross Road; Frances Mary Herbert. Seated on the left of the front row is Nellie Herbert.

Timber being transported by Coltman Bros, using a traction engine, from Hanslope Park, 1930s.

A painting of Green End Farm, Hanslope, 1880. The farm was purchased by Joseph Knibb, the well-known clockmaker, in 1691. He had originally set up business in London and Oxford before retiring to Hanslope. He died in 1711 and clocks bearing his Hanslop signature are rare. The house, which had mullion windows, was down the lane by the school and across fields. Eventually empty and vandalised, it was demolished some years ago.

This 6 ft 5 in tall antique clock, made by Joseph Knibb, was sold at Sotheby's when it was nearly 300 years old. Described as a small walnut marquetry case clock, it bore the signature 'Joseph Knibb at Hanslop' and was expected to fetch between £8,000 and £12,000. It had inlays of flowers, five ringed pillars and a shaped calendar aperture. On the left is a close-up of the face, encircled by four cherubs.

Hanslope's Grand Village Fayre, June 1979. Michael Burbidge, left (in character as Irishman Simon Byrne) and Andy Barnes (as Alexander McKay, champion of Scotland) re-enact the renowned bare-knuckle prize fight which took place on Salcey Green, 2 June 1830, for £100 a side. After forty-seven rounds McKay was carried away unconscious, and died the next day, aged twenty-six. There is a famous tombstone poem in Hanslope churchyard. Simon Byrne was arrested at Liverpool on board the Dublin packet, tried for manslaughter but acquitted. McKay died from compression of the brain, according to James Heygate, a surgeon living in Hanslope who bled him. Illegal since 1750, the last prize fight to be held in England was Tom Sayers v. John Heenan on Farnborough Common, Hampshire, 17 April 1860.

Hanslope St James AFC, champions of the Bucks League, Division II, 1906/7 and 1907/8. Back row, left to right: A. Ditum, H. Neale. Second row: F. Sawbridge, T. Herbert, H. Brownsell, O. Mills, G. Horn. Third row: J. Kerridge, A. Olney, W. Stimson, F. Elkington. Front row: W. Woodland, T. Chilton, F. Kerridge, H. Simons, A. Green. The man standing on the left of the photo is Alf Sawbridge, father of Jack Sawbridge, who was a well-known cattle dealer.

Hanslope Welfare, *c.* 1953. Back row, left to right: Clarice Tebbutt, Dorothy Horne with David, Phyllis Wilson, Derrie Eakins with John, ? Sharp with Caroline, Doreen Richards with Peter. Second row: -?-, Christine Branson, ? Sawbridge with Clive, Barbara Bellham with Susan, Rita Boss with Michael, the doctor (name not known), ? Hall, Heather Sedgwick with Nigel, ? Shakespeare, Mrs Cooper (village doctor's wife), Mavis Jubb, Miss A. Turney, district nurse (hidden), Vera Rookes, Mary Pickett, ? Rock, Bessie Gable, Gwen Haynes, Elsie Campbell. Third row: ? Clarke with twin girls, Enid Scarsbrook with Peter, Millie Wells with Jeremy, Beulah Chilton with Marilyn, ? Rock, Iris Baker with Malcolm and David, Ruth Mobley with Peggy, Sylvia Mobley with Richard, Miss Lines, health visitor. Front row: ? Wilson, Pat Rookes, Barry Sharp, ? Clarke, Barbara Horne, Richard Campbell, Gary Rock, Trevor Tebbutt, Pat Mobley, Edward Branson, Paul Sedgwick, Michael Jubb, Sheriden Keech, Pamela Haynes.

On her milk round for John Webb of Long Street Farm, Hanslope, is Mercy with 'Jack' the horse, *c.* 1916. Although he only had a milk round in Hanslope, he was a 'high stepper', and could get to Northampton, a distance of 10 miles, in an hour.

After Frank H. Bellham retired from his bus service, which he ran from 1920 to 1959, he specialised in growing sweet peas as a hobby and won many prizes, including the Astbury Cup eight times between 1950 and 1968. He is pictured with it here. Frank won the Duffield Trophy seven times for sweet peas at Northampton Show, and also exhibited at the National Sweet Pea Society shows in London and from Southampton to Liverpool, including Bath, Cheltenham and Nottingham, and won prizes for flowers and vegetables at local shows in the area.

Ted Ditum of Hanslope, born 1902 and photographed with his parents, William and Mary Ann (Molly) Ditum, *c.* 1937. The picture shows prizes and some of the gold medals he won. He ran for WAAC, District Railway London, Northampton Athletic Club and London Polytechnic. His trainer was Arthur Ditum. Ted achieved a remarkable amount of success: 9 July 1921: Wolverton the first winners of the Bucks County Shield: 2nd in Junior 880 yds; April 1922: 3rd in 2¼-mile race around grass oval, Wolverton Park; 1924: Represented Wolverton in the Kettering and Northampton Road Relay; 1925: 6th in first race of the Cross Country Season; 1926: One of the only two individual winners for Wolverton in the Bucks AAA's Championships 880 yds.

The entrance to the village of Castlethorpe from Haversham, *c.* 1898. Nowadays the view is similar but the two houses are no longer thatched and the road has been widened to accommodate modern traffic. Between the hedge and cottage on the right is Bullington End Road. The girl standing on the left is a Nichols; the other little girl is Elsie Burbidge, aged about four.

North Bucks Dance Festival, Castlethorpe Primary School, 1951. The photograph includes Clifford Ray, Stuart Lane, John Cooper, Carole Bavington, Susie Robinson, Maureen Collyer, John Synnott, Jean Pittam, Maureen Synnott, Richard King, Carole Keeves, Ann Gray and Dorothy Belton.

Castlethorpe Primary School PE group, spring 1951. The girls are in their gym kit – their vests and knickers! They are seen with their sports equipment minus a few tree logs. Back row, left to right: Glenys Collyer, Maureen Collyer, Shelagh Meachem, Anne Gray. Second row: Jennifer Hart, Daphne Harper, Amy Booth, Susie Robinson, Josie Lane, John Cooper, Peter Thomas, Rodney White, Greerson Gower. Third row: Carol Stevens, Christine Ward, Lesley Bates, Maureen Synnott, Jean Pittam, Dorothy Belton, Carole Keeves, Clifford Ray. Fourth row: David Scripps, John Synnott, Thomas Hart, Tony Collyer, Dick Ray, Stuart Lane, Adrian Pittam, Richard Hart. Front row: Rodney Harper, Aiden Cook, Reginald Gregory, Roy West, Richard King, Linda Harper.

A celebration of the King's Coronation given on 23 August 1902: '2,030 years' are represented by twenty-nine villagers of Castlethorpe at a tea given at Langton House.

Yardley Gobion School football team, 1928. Back row, left to right: Albert Horton, Kenneth Hepworth, Joe Swain, Ted Whiting, Geoffrey Holton, Gordon Wotherspoon, Jack Key (trainer, killed in Cyprus during the Second World War). Front row: Alf Horton, Tom Kightley, George Glenn, Maurice Swain, Stan Church.

Yardley Gobion May Day, 1932. Back row, left to right: John Odell, Olive Holton, Ivy Durrant, Dennis Atkins. In the centre: May Queen Dorothy Horton. Second row: Molly Kightley, a boy from Botany Bay, Eileen Kightley (retiring Queen), Vera Atkins, ? Pettifer (from Botany Bay), Winnie Durrant. Third row: Doris Johnson, Peggy Burkett, Jean Swain. Front row: Mamie Cross, John Evans, George Barker, Gladys Fenn.

May Day country dancing, the 'Butterfly Dance', 1931. Left to right: Gert Glenn, Rosie Evans, Maud Swain, Ivy Durrant, Doll Horton. Eileen Kightley (front, centre) was reprimanded for not looking at her butterfly!

Potterspury Rose Queen, 1938. A variety of costumes are included here: Joy Pattimore was 'Sun', Kath Owen was 'Rain' and six were flowers. Back row, left to right: Eileen Holloway, Fred Langley, Jean Jefcoate, Ron Spencer, Eric Walters, Viv Tapp, Eric Warren, Joy Pattimore, Olive Webster, Kath Henson, Joyce Hughes (Rose Queen), Coral Stewart, Winnie Russell, Pat Dunkley, Doll Atkins, Yvonne Lambert, Peggy Smith, Bill Bryan, -?-, Bob Tapp. Second row: Pat Packer, Sylvia Onan, -?-, Audrey Meakins, Doug Holloway, Phyllis Barby, Rose Barby, Maureen Russell, Syd Tapp, Pete Meakins, Gillian Tapp, -?-, -?-, -?-, -?-, Margaret Evans. Third row: Norah Davies, -?-, -?-, Margaret Holloway, Hazel Howe, -?-, Mavis Holloway, Sheila Holloway, Patsy Henson, -?-, Betty Bazeley, -?-, Doll Jefcoate, Nellie Langley, -?-, Iris Stewart. Front row: -?-, Donald Palmer, -?-, Harold Jefcoate, -?-, Terry Howard, -?-, Johnny Nightingale. Standing on right: -?-, Ruth Henson, Trevor Lambert.

A group of Women's Institute ladies outside Potterspury Hall, Rose Queen Day, 1938. Left to right: Mrs Jess Bradbury, Mrs Sinclair, Nancy Tarry, Mrs Mary Tapp, Maud Green, Mrs Cowley, Mrs Sue Onan, Mrs Maycock. Seated in the centre: Dorothy Pratt.

Mr and Mrs Fairchild in their motorised tricar, late nineteenth or early twentieth century. They lived at The Cottage, Poundfield Road, Potterspury, and Mr Fairchild is believed to have been the agent for the Duke of Grafton who sold his local estates in the early 1920s. He later collected rents all around the village, on a bicycle, for Towcester Rural District Council.

A delightful photo of the Wootton family, Potterspury, 1948. Left to right: Eleanor (4), Alex (7), Michael (6 months), Dennis (2) and Tony (5½).

Doug Holloway standing on the footbridge over the ford in Blackwell End, Potterspury, mid-1930s. Thatched cottages stood where the Council bungalows now stand.

Cock Inn outing, Potterspury, late 1940s. Back row, left to right: Frank Horton, Arthur Wootton, Frank Holloway, Basil Richards, Arthur Henson, Charlie Terry, Jack Swain, Harry Tapp, Mr Twisleton, Jimmy Milne, Albert Ratcliffe, Dick Tapp, Henry Stewart, -?-, Harry Jefcoate, Albert Webster, Joe Ratcliffe. Middle row: Harry Meakins (in raincoat), Sydney Holloway, Jack Luck (landlord, Cock Inn), Herbert Russell, Archie Bushell, Levi Tapp, Albert Evans, Joe Warren. Front row: Jack Williams, Bill Tapp, Bill Henson, Horace Prosser, Doug Evans, Cyril Lawson, Bill Druce.

Potterspury Women's Institute, *c.* 1965. Back row, left to right: Phyllis Russell, Kath Young, Ann Brown, Jean Carroll. Second row: May Duffy, -?-, Joan Duffy, Doreen Beaton, Gwen Soper, -?-, June Eglesfield, Jean Roy, Mrs Richmond-Watson. Third row: Cis Wootton, Ada Henson, Nell Wootton, ? Sinclaire, Mary Tapp, Alice Evans, Margaret Powell, Lucy Henson, Mary Russell. Fourth row: Ciss Lambert, Gladys Barby, Kathleen Prosser, Marjorie Hall, Betty Tapp, Vera Rose, Olive Duckmanton. Front row: a pupil at Pury Lodge, another pupil at Pury Lodge, Betty Wordell.

Potterspury Football Club, 1934/5. They were champions of the North Bucks League, Division I, winners of the Stantonbury Hospital Cup, winners of the South Northants Medals Competition, and semi-finalists of the Buckingham Hospital Cup. Back row, left to right: G. Knibbs (committee), W. Perkins (Auditor), P.H. Leadbeater (Chairman), A. Barby (committee), T. Pratt (Auditor). Second row: H. Evans (committee), W. Lambert (committee), W.H. Lampard (Secretary), R.G. Rickson, J.C. McEachran, W. Ratcliffe, W.H. Henson, J. Nightingale (Asst Trainer), C.H. Webster (Treasurer), D. Kerr (committee). Third row: G. Brown (Trainer), O.G. Osborne, A.E. Henson, W.G. Atkins, A. Evans (Captain), Capt. B. Gratton-Holt (President), A. Giles (Vice-Captain), C. Pettifer, W.A. Wootton, J. Meakins, R. Pettifer. Front row: A.H. Birdsay, K. Holloway, D. Evans, H. Postlethwaite, W.G. Toombs, A. Henson, S. Boswell. The photograph was taken outside 'The Mansion', Potterspury House, home of Capt. and Mrs Gratton-Holt.

Opposite, above: Potterspury School choir, March 1935 – winners of the Schilizzi Cup and Davis Cup at Northampton Eisteddfod. Back row, left to right: Reg Lambert, Les Meakins, Joyce Hughes, Hazel Tarry, Mary Tapp, Winnie Russell, Marie Ballinger, Kath Henson, Malcolm Owen, Charles Meakins. Second row: Rosemarie Henson, Joan Lampard, Norah Tapp, Rose Richardson, Mr P.H. Leadbeater (Headmaster), Milly Henson, Alfreda Webster, Brenda Tarry, Rene Onan. Third row: Reg Onan, Jean Brown, Roy Evans (holding cup), Gordon Tapp (holding cup) Avril Brown, Ken Barby. Front row: Geoffrey Twistleton, Dorothy Jeffcoate, Bernard Walker (holding certificate), Ken Baud, Vivian Tapp (holding certificate), Arnold Owen.

Opposite, below: Potterspury County School, 1950. Back row, left to right: Philip Ward, Ann Webster, Geoffrey Holloway, Geoffrey Meakins, Timothy Pettifer, Ivan Smith, Angela Coppin, Edwina Cotterell. Second row: George Bullock, Maurice Lambert, Rosemary Weston, Brian Collard, David Owen, Shirley Atkins, Martin Richards, Jean Osborne, Gordon Henson, Victor Meakins. Third row: Elizabeth Joad, Vera Howerd, Dennis Wootton, Alan Bright, Sheila Atkins, Nora Crowder, later Mrs Horton (teacher), Marlene Barby, Peter Cox, Victor Francis, Margaret Bushell, Jean Partridge. Front row: Derek Howerd, Denis Wright, John Trew, Roy Tapp, Michael Wootton.

MID NORTHAMPTONSHIRE
MUSICAL + COMPETITION
CONDUCTOR
DATE
MID NORTHAMPTONSHIRE
MUSICAL + COMPETITION

Children's New Year's party given by the Rector, the Revd H.N.C. Hewson at Cosgrove Rectory, 4 January 1940. The rector was a little man, only about 5 ft tall, and was known in the village as 'Little Jackie'. He stood on a fish box in the pulpit! Back row, left to right: Audrey Ruff, Beryl Tompkins, Eric Meakins, George Hill, Joan Lord, Daphne Kingston, Ray Meakins, David Brown. Second row: Margaret Hitchcock, Mrs Hewson with her dog Snap, Christopher Whitaker, Cynthia Tompkins, John Loughrey, Gladys Loughrey, Peggy Ruff, Peter Brown, Betty Hillyer, Joan Peach, Doug Hillyer, Peter Whitaker. Third row: Marina Whitaker, Pauline Bushell, the Revd H.N.C. Hewson, Peggy Hillier, Edith Waite. Front row: Winnie Waite, Reggie Waite, Bob Gallop, Geoff Williams, Donald Kightley, Jean Loughrey, Dennis Tompkins.

Jim Lambert, Cosgrove, *c.* 1946. Jim was a keen apiarist for over twenty-five years, and was a member of the Wolverton Beekeepers Association. As a church bellringer he rang Quarter Peals with teams of bellringing beekeepers for the Royal Show at Stoneleigh. He kept twenty hives in the Rectory grounds, and these once provided good food for several broods of nightingales, bred in the nearby double hedge. The young nightingales sat on the hives and picked off the bees as they flew in.

A bellringers' outing organised by Fred Tustain, Cosgrove, 1950s. In the bus doorway: Olive Johnson and Mrs Louis Cadwell. Left to right: Edie Sharp (Tyringham), Reg Evans (Newport Pagnell), Louis Cadwell (Hanslope), Cecil Sharp (Gayhurst), Bob Abraham (Newport Pagnell), Fred Tustain, Edie Daniels, Reg Howson (Newport Pagnell), Mrs Billy Dillow, Mrs Bert Edwards, Bert Edwards (Stony Stratford), Tommy Trasler (Stony Stratford), -?-, Billy Dillow (Stony Stratford), -?-, Vic Adams (Weston Underwood), Hedley Tustain, John Higgins, Mrs Vic Adams, Mrs Bushell (Barley Mow, Cosgrove), Mrs Hedley Tustain, Mrs Gascoigne, Mrs Fred Case, Fred Case (Wicken), Reg Bailey (Beachampton). (Photograph by Bert (Algie) Daniels)

The first Village Hall committee at Cosgrove, 1948. The ground for the hall was given by Capt. P.Y. Atkinson of The Priory. Back row, left to right: Arthur Loughrey, George Hickford, Bob Gallop, Dick Lavington, Fred Tustain, Tom Kightley. Front row: Harry Cummings, Reg Whiting, Frank Hillier, Jack Hebson, Joe Jones, Olive Johnson, Jack Johnson.

A party for the children of the village of Cosgrove at the opening of the first Village Hall, *c.* 1949. Aren't they spellbound watching the magic lantern show! The rear of the group includes Jim Holman, Dolly Williams, Mrs Nora Horton, Vera Stewart, Susan Coles, Tony Lavington, Sylvia Wickham, Louie Gascoigne, Jessie Stewart, Sheila Brown, Rosemary Hebson. The front includes Jo Hebson, Ivor Hickford, Carol Prater, Pauline Bushell, Julie Longman, Jill Tustain, Jill Hebson, Sue Tustain and June Smith.

Cosgrove School, 1889 or 1890. In the second row from the back are three brothers: second, third and fourth from the left, Monty Henson, Fred Henson, Ben Henson. At this time people had to count to ten and not move before the photograph was taken to prevent blurring. (Photograph by Bartholomew of Great Linford)

Henry William Lambert and his wife Eliza Flowers, a widow, formerly Miss Cadd, in their Sunday best, *c.* 1900. They were married at Yardley Gobion on 8 August 1881. The photograph was taken at the kissing gate near the Barlow Mow public house. They lived nearby at 4 Blacksmiths Yard, now a car park.

A typical scene outside Cosgrove Mill, *c.* 1880. Thomas Amos, a farmer and maltster from Castle Thorpe, has sent corn to be ground at the mill. Mr Brinson was living in the cottage on the left at the time, and may be the gentleman on the right with his son.

The staff at Cosgrove Hall, *c.* 1934. Their employers were Mr and Mrs G.H. Winterbotham. Back row, left to right: Bill Pebody (chauffeur), Alf Whitaker (gardener), Evelyn Payne (chambermaid), Elsie ?, later Mrs Horace Parkinson (cook), Ernest C. Lambert (head gardener), Jim Lambert (garden boy). Front row: Ivy Hopcroft (parlourmaid), George Hooton (general duties), Ellie ? (kitchen maid). George Hooton was seriously wounded in the throat by shrapnel during the First World War, and could only speak in a whisper.

Cosgrove Football Club, champions of Division II, 1947/8. Back row, left to right: Jimmy Burrows (landlord, Plough Inn, Cosgrove), Archie Bushell, John Shervington (Goalie), -?-, Peter Brown. Middle row: Bill Ratcliffe (Trainer), Arthur Loughrey, Howard Smith, Ray Meakins, Les Markham, Albert Tompkins, Percy Swain. Front row: David Brown, Eric Meakins, Freddie Herbert, Capt. P.Y. Atkinson (President) of The Priory, Cosgrove, Harry Cummings, Tom Kightley, John Nightingale.

Fishing on the Buckingham Arm, the Cosgrove Road side of the Grand Union Canal, 1950s. Left to right: Mr Albert Nichols, Eric Rance, Mr Harry Rance (a hairdresser from Stony Stratford; his shop was on the left-hand side of the Cock Hotel, and is now a bar) and Ralph Nichols. They were members of the Stony Stratford Angling Club and fished from Old Stratford to the first bridge towards Cosgrove on Buckingham Arm, but the photograph was taken on the towpath side.

Cosgrove Women's Institute at their twenty-first birthday party, some members in fancy dress, showing the cake made by their Correspondent in New Zealand during the Second World War. Note the bare table, depicting food shortages. Back row, left to right: Olive Johnson, Ena Lavington, Lil Longman, Doll Hebson, Myrtle Barby, Marion Freestone, Doris Smith, Lizzie Stewart, -?-, Dora Clark, Muriel Ratledge. Second row: Mrs 'Nebo' Davis, WIHQ representative, Mary Hillyer, Rose Rickaby, Phil Loughrey. Third row: Louie Castle, -?-, -?-, Mrs Frank Chown, Mrs Percy Lyman, Win Harris, Gertrude Marlow, Ruby Kitson, Florrie Castle, Dora Fiel, Mrs Gascoigne, Nellie Whitaker, Mrs Bert Tack. Front row: Kath Jones, Gracie Atkinson, Mabel Jelley (President), Mrs Reg Whiting, Joan Brockway.

Albert Edward Chapman outside the business he started in Cosgrove Road, Old Stratford. He was later joined by his sons Arthur Edward and Sidney Harold Chapman and the business became A.E. Chapman & Sons. They took over the business on the retirement of their father on 4 April 1946 under the title A.E. & S.H. Chapman. They were wheelwrights and agricultural engineers, making wheels for carts and repairing cattle wagons. Arthur retired in about 1970. The business has now closed.

David Jones (Headmaster of the British School, Stony Stratford) with his wife Mary Ann 'Minnie' Smith, standing outside their home, Wharf House, Old Stratford, with their family, *c.* 1918. Both were from Worcester. Left to right: Dora (who married Walter Mackerness, chemist, Wolverton) with her daughter, 'Little Dora', Eric Jones (in chair), Joe Jones (on lap), Minnie (who married Jim Payne of Paynes' Coaches), Evelyn (who married Archie Dormer, Headmaster of Russell Street School, Stony Stratford). Harold Jones was absent: he was away in the army as a result of the First World War.

'Little Dora' Mackerness taking her doll for a walk. Her grandparents' home, Wharf House, Old Stratford, is in the background. David Jones, her grandfather, also owned the three brick cottages nearby and Dora lived in the one nearest to Wharf House. She later married Lewis Clark. Dora was a WI member for many years and held pillowlace-making classes at her home in Clarence Road, Stony Stratford.

Roy Hills whizzing down Mounthill Avenue, Old Stratford, on his roller skates, 1950s. Roy's home was 6 Mounthill Avenue.

In 1961 Deanshangar & Wicken British Legion presented the village of Deanshanger with an ornate seat, cast from wrought-iron. In 1987, more than twenty-five years on and after being repaired and renovated, it was resited away from the main road – and six of those committee members from 1961 turned out. Left to right: Bob Marshall, Fred Hamson, John Marshall, Eric Darby (Treasurer), Joe Read and Steve Chaytor (Secretary). Sadly three of the members have since died: the President, Mr J. James, the Vice-President, Tommy Easteal and the Chairman, Wal Taylor.

Men of the Deanshangar RAOB (Royal Antediluvian Order of Buffaloes) Lodge No. 1863. This was started by Stan Ball in about 1952. They met in the Rose & Crown public house. Back row, left to right: Les Drinkwater, 'Curly' Tapp, Albert Andrews, Gerald Andrews, Cyril Tapp, Stan Ball (founder), Derek Smith, Ted Whittemore, Gerald Tapp, Bob Stacey, Bert Robinson, George Clarke. Front row: Johnnie Evans, Den Wiley, Steve Chaytor, Tom Canvin.

Ladies of the 'Buffs' (Deanshanger RAOB), 1950s. Back row, left to right: Mrs Pratt with Wendy, Mrs Canvin, Jean Phillips, Lou King, Phyllis Andrews, Vera Drinkwater, Mrs A. Andrews, Helen Tapp, Joan Smith, Joyce Chaytor with Alan. Front row: Isabel Davies with Paul, Glad Andrews with Alan or Morrell, Ena Stacey, Joan Whittemore, Mrs Canvin, P. Ball, Mrs Pratt, Gill King.

Kay Brazier, who was Deanshanger May Queen in 1959, with her attendants. Left to right: Steven Marshall, Carol Tovey, Maureen Nicholls, Barbara Boots.

Holy Trinity Church Choir, Deanshanger, *c*. 1963. Back row, left to right: Mrs Olive Fielding, -?-, Mrs Mann, Mrs Archie Reynolds, Miss May Capel, Dora Nicholls, Mrs Evelyn Heppinstall, Joan Crossan. Second row: Darryl Case, Robert (Bob) Fielding, Ernie Baker, Gerald Godfrey, Ben Wanoa, Bill Boots. Third row: Stella Taylor, Christine Webb, Patricia Godfrey, Christine Williams, Sheila Godfrey, Barbara Boots, -?-, the Revd Albert Bransby. Front row: Lynne Godfrey, Lesley Reynolds, -?-, Carol Webster, Helen Boots, Yvonne Bull, Alison Tompkins.

Three of the pupils from the Pamela James School of Dancing, 1940s. Left to right: Rosamond Hall, Miriam Waters (as Bo-Peep), Ann Knibbs. Pamela James was born in Essex and arrived in Deanshanger during the Second World War after her home was bombed. She started the dancing school when only fifteen years of age and gave variety shows and pantomimes in Potterspury, Akeley, Yardley Gobion, Cosgrove, Great Horwood and Deanshanger throughout the war, for charities such as the Duke of Gloucester's Red Cross Fund, Potterspury Comforts Fund, the Prisoner of War Comforts Fund and Northampton General Hospital.

Hard luck – he didn't win this raffle prize! Harry Canvin's younger brother Trevor is in the aluminium plane that was the main raffle prize at an event held in Mrs Walter Cattell's garden, Deanshanger, *c.* 1948. She supported many good causes.

Deanshanger Cricket Club, early 1950s. They were winners of the *Wolverton Express* Knock-out Cup. Wolverton provided umpires in a final. Back row, left to right: Leo Bostock (Wolverton), Dave Hill, Pete Henson, John Tompkins, Sid Bird, Ben Bull, Gordon Roberts, Dennis Read, Archie Buswell, Harold 'Dill' Jones, Pete Wyatt (scorer), Nigel Smith. Front row: George Lea, Len Bellamy, Brian Leete, Gerald Godfrey (Captain and Secretary, with cup), Les Roberts, Buryl Church, Roger Smith.

Fishing Awards, April 1968. Presentations to members of the Deanshanger and Old Stratford Angling Association were made during a social in the Memorial Hall, Deanshanger. Mr Derek Lawson presented trophies to Cyril Mallows (centre), and other winners. Left to right: Mr J. Timms, Mr M. Holt, Martin Hall, Brian Roff, Mr E. Longhurst.

Deanshanger School, winners at the Northampton Eisteddfod, *c.* 1933. Back row, left to right: Mr Taylor–Brown (Headmaster), George Pratt, Cyril King, Ben Bull, Doug Goldney, Frank Savage, Francis Nicholls, Les Drinkwater. Second row: Mabel Bull, Doris Ridgway, Kathleen Pryor, Phyllis Harris, ? Holman, Muriel Barby, Isabel Davies, Joan Varney, Miss Caroline Bradley (teacher). Front row: Helen Tapp, ? Holman, Lorna Roberts, Elsie Nicholls, Joan Grant, Betty Ridgway, Louie Andrews, Sheila Tapp, Yvonne Robinson.

Deanshanger County School, 1955. Back row, left to right: Michael Russell, Harold Watts, Ted Miller, Bob Sapwell, John Holmes, David Taylor, Dennis Nicholls, Tony Walton, Brian Hollis. Second row: Linda Ward, Ann Morgan, Jill Burrows, Jill Foddy, Joan Dumbleton, Mary Bazeley, Carol Green, Pat Barby, Wendy Darby, June Law. Third row: Michael Green, Alan Andrews, Bobby Errington, Doug Knibbs, Christine Millward, Charles Pascoe (teacher), Celia Brignall, Brian Robinson, Michael Boyes, Arthur Gray, Alan Bull. Front row: Valerie Foddy, Tony Green, Roy Smith, Michael Barby, Shaun King, Leonard Simmons, Olive Bunker.

Deanshanger School's *Cinderella*, *c.* 1920. This photo was taken in the paint shop of E. & H. Roberts' Foundry; the Roberts family were very active in the local community. Back row, left to right: Blanche Roberts, Phyllis Roberts (witch), May Austin. Middle row: Doris Wyatt, Margaret Bailey, Doris Bailey, Clara Russell, Minnie Church, Molly Canvin, Rose Tolley, Olive Smith. Front row: Dora Stretton, -?- (Prince Charming), Pearl Parry, Edie Barby, Evelyn Barby.

Wicken Cricket Club, *c.* 1902. Back row, second from left: George Green snr, father of Albert John Green. Seated, second from left: Albert John (Jack) Green snr, father of J.A. Green. Lounging on the right: Fred Case. Note the scoreboard in the background: 174 all out, 10 wickets, 4 runs last man.

Wicken Women's Institute on an outing to Penrhyn Castle, Bangor, North Wales, 1926. At that time Lord and Lady Penrhyn were the landowners of Wicken, and resided at Wicken Park. Back row, left to right: Pearl Ward, Dot Jackson, Mrs Marchant, Mrs Fred Starsmore, Mary Case, Miss Daisy Hurst (Stony Stratford), -?-, Phyllis Capel, Betty Jackson, bus driver, Miss I. Tyrell. Middle row: Edie Ward, Mrs Williams, Edie Barby, -?-, Lizzie James, Mrs W. Starsmore, -?-, Mrs Wrighton, Mrs Chexfield, Kate Robinson, Dorothy Atkins, -?- (from Stony Stratford), Mrs Haynes, -?- (from Stony Stratford), Mrs Garner, -?-, Mrs Green, Mrs Pitson. Front row: Milly Ward, Mrs Plummer, G. Eden, Mrs Keylock.

A nice Wicken country scene, *c.* 1938. It shows the Four Elms planted in 1709, which were sadly cut down during the Second World War by Whattons of Hartwell: the trunks were taken away, while the tops were used locally for firewood. The house Elm Bank is on the left of the photograph.

The sundial above the front door of Elm Bank, 6 Leckhampstead Road, Wicken, home of Jessie and Cyril Eden. It is inscribed 'Memorandum y thofe 4 Elms was planted on this hill in FeB. 1709 by RW AC & RB'. (Photo by Audrey Lambert)

The golden wedding of William and Mary Ann Barby of Wicken, celebrating with their five sons and four daughters and their families, 1930. Back row, left to right: Bill Janes (Nellie's son), Will Barby (son), Polly (Will's wife), May (daughter), Nellie (daughter), Ted Barby (son), Lotte (wife of Ted), Dolly (daughter), Dick Dennis (Annie's husband), Alec Barby (son), Florrie (wife of Aubrey), ? Bird (husband of Dolly), Ron Barby (Will's son), Aubrey Barby (son). Middle row: George Barby (son), Mary Ann Barby, William Barby, Annie Barby (daughter). Front row: Don Bird, Phil Bird, Jim Bird (three of Dolly's children). (Photo taken by Aubrey Barby)

Mrs Bess Barby of Wicken sawing wood for her fire, *c.* 1900.

A group of bellringers from towers around north Buckinghamshire and south Northamptonshire, *c.* 1933. Back row, left to right: Harry Ridgeway, Bert Gibbons, Freddie Case, Ernest C. Lambert, Bill Clark, John Higgings, -?-, -?-, Vic Adams, George Cooper, Cyril Warner, -?-, Len Smith. Middle row: Harry Hurst, Jack Green, Tommy Tompkins, George Green snr, Freddie Pateman, Tommy Roberts, Billy Neale. Front row: Edwin R. (Ted) Lambert, George Green, Frank Green, Jim Green.

A visitor to the village of Wicken enjoys his tankard of ale at the 'Cake and Ale' on Ascension Day, 1938. The 413th celebration of the unification of Wyke Hamon and Wyke Dyve, which gave us Wicken as we know it today, took place on 1 June 2000. A hundred people attended a service in the church of St John the Evangelist, led by the Bishop of Peterborough, the Rt Revd Ian Cundy, followed by a thanksgiving at the site of the Gospel Elm, ending with all partaking of 'Cake and Ale' in the village hall. This year the event was seen on television and broadcast on the radio.

A delightful watercolour painting of Cross Tree Road, Wicken, *c.* 1890. The artist was the brother of Mrs Perridge who painted it on a visit to his sister, who later gave it as a wedding present to Edith Clara Giles, the great-aunt of Ann Foddy. The lady near the wall is Mrs Fanny Green, owner of the bakehouse shop (seen in the distance on the left), who was blind; the other lady is Mrs Carpenter. The Spencer coat of arms can be seen on the reading room on the left.

Wicken village pound was usually maintained by either the manor or the vestry. It is a very rare surviving example of its type. John Marchant unveiled a plaque on behalf of the Wicken Conservation Society on Saturday 12 June 1999. He provided a railway sleeper for the plinth. The plaque reads 'Within these walls, straying horses, cattle and other animals were "impounded" and released by the owner after paying the fine incurred.' (Photo by Audrey Lambert)

Wicken Club Day centenary, 1938. The Victoria Club was run by the Wicken Medical and Benefits Society. The flagbearer is Tom Read. The Cross Tree can be seen in the distance, and on the left is the cart outside the bakehouse where the roasted meat was cooked in Bertie Wrightson's bread oven. It was then transported to the school hall where the men had lunch, waited on by the ladies. There was a tea for women and children. They paraded right through the village ending at Meurig-Davies' Home Farm, where his wife served drinks to members of Bradwell Band, who led the parade every year. Favourite tunes were 'Colonel Bogey' and 'Shade the Donkey'.

Wicken Club Feast, 1938. This was always held on the Tuesday at Whitsuntide. The men were given Churchwarden clay pipes, and here some of them are posing for a photograph. Left to right: Mr Hughes, Frank Ward, Arthur Hurst, Tom Barby, Jim Ward, Wallace Taylor, Ron Bunker, Hubert Brown, Ted Cooper, Alec Barby, Ron Bunker, George Hurst, Richard Hurst (organist at St John's Church).

Wicken Club Day, 1938. The ladies and children, who enjoyed a sumptuous tea. Back row, left to right: Mrs Jackson, Mrs Ward, Mrs Vellacott snr, Miss Edie Ward, Mrs Cashmore, Mrs Frank Ward, Mrs Parry, Mrs Henson, Mrs Will Starsmore, Mrs George Barby, -?-, Miss Sibthorpe (Stony Stratford), Mrs Tom Read, Iris Cowley. Middle row: Mrs Wright, Doris Smith, Mrs Meurig-Davies, Vera Vellacott, Mrs Reynolds, Mrs Jim Ward with Betty, Mrs Plummer, Mrs Eden with child on lap, Mrs York Cooper. Front row: -?-, Peter Cowley, -?-, ? Barby (Deanshanger).

The winning tug-o'-war team at Wicken Club Day, 1936 or 1937. Back row, left to right: ? Neesham, Bill Collett, Tom Read, Alan Carter, Fred Bateman, George Pitson, Bill Harding. Front row: Ted Lucas, Walt Jackson (publican at the White Lion), Bert Robinson.

Wicken School in Coronation year, 1953. Back row, left to right: Olive Bunker, Stella Odam, Joan Birdsey, Doreen Walton, Janice Case, Brenda Jones, Patricia Forbes, Peter Tansley. Middle row: Bobby Errington, Mrs Lees (teacher), Brian Green, Roy Pitson, Albert Pitson, Arthur Gray, Terry Cashmore, John Folker, Keith Pitson, Tony Walton, Michael Green. Front row: Josephine Ivens, Tony Green, Marylyn Errington, Alan Gray, Lesley Tansley, Richard Ivens, Lynne Portlock, Derek Bunker, Margaret Birdsey, Leslie Holt, Constance Errington.

The first of three nonagenarians in her family was Mrs Thos Gray of Wicken making pillowlace aged ninety-three, *c.* 1913. She had a daughter living in Wicken in 1942, also aged ninety-three. Mrs Gray was the great-aunt of Mrs Gladys Eden, who was ninety-eight on 1 July 2000 and is Wicken's oldest resident. She has a very clear memory and was invaluable when naming the ladies in the WI photograph on page 75.

A peaceful country scene on a hot summer's day, early 1950s. Hens are scratching for food in the dried-up pond, which had gone by the 1930s, and a trap rounds the corner in Lower Weald, Calverton. The cottages, while still there, are no longer thatched.

Coronation day, 2 June 1953. This is one of four photographs taken of the villagers of Calverton, who enjoyed a celebration meal in the barn at Mr Fountain's Manor Farm. The couple on the camera side of the nearest table: Mary Webb and Bob Webb snr. Left: Bob Webb jnr. Those facing the camera on the nearest table are: Doug Jones, Molly Webb, Bett Jones with Liz, Mr Knight, Mrs Knight, Les Gerrard and his son, Mrs George, Rosetta Knight now Mrs Gerrard. Standing, left: Billy Wilkes. Those at the back include: Wal Poynter, Mrs Poynter, Jean Poynter, Pat Hillyer and Denise Hillyer, Mrs Taylor, Barbara Taylor, Stuart Taylor, Bill Hill, Mrs Hill, Brian Edwards, Mrs Davis, Ron Missenden, Mr Hill and Bill Scripps.

Pupils at Calverton village school, *c*. 1923. They are with their teacher, Cissie Tompkins, who died shortly afterwards; all the children had to attend her funeral. They were in tears as they sang a rather morbid hymn by Mrs Alexander (Ancient & Modern no. 575) which commences: 'Within the churchyard side by side are many long low graves . . .'. The school closed in 1926. Back row, left to right: Cissie Tompkins, Ted Leonard, Fred Neal, Albert Bazeley, Arthur Goodger. Second row: -?-, Nellie Goodger, Winnie Leonard, Eileen Roberts, Nellie Sims. Front row: Eileen West, Kathleen Roberts, Marjorie Goodger, Florence Wilmin, Dora Bazeley, Gladys Goodger, Olive Bryant.

Watery Lane, Beachampton, living up to its name, in flood, June 1983. The Land Rover belonged to Rodney Corner, the present Milton Keynes coroner. Max Morley, who is in the vehicle, put a rope across it to pull it out. Liz Smalley is watching the operation from the far bank.

Council roadmen placing a new layer of tarmacadam on the road in Nash, 1930s. They are grouped around their steam-roller, which probably dates from the 1920s. Some of these steam-rollers were in service for some forty years, until the late 1960s.

The boys and girls of Whaddon in the recreation ground, with Keith Birch on his motorbike, 1945. Left to right: Bob West, Edward Justice, Leslie Tofield, John Hopkins, Ross Williss, Dennis Gardner, Keith Birch and Harry Adams (on motorbike), Shirley Litchfield, Kath Wrighton.

This block of houses was known as 'Coronation Street'! They were photographed in 1906 when the area was known as The Common or Pink's End, probably named after Parson Pink, as the vicarage is situated at the end of the road. By about 1935 it was renamed Vicarage Road, but today the vicarage is known as Whaddon House.

Cricket Club dinner, Whaddon, 1949 or 1950. Front row, left to right: the Revd Basil Chalenor, -?-, -?-, Mr Twelvetree (Cricket Club Secretary), James Reece (from Padbury), Mrs Duke, Mr Duke. Left to right by wall: Mr Dormer, Mrs Dormer, Mr Wrighton, Mrs Wrighton, Mrs D. Torner, Miss Parrott, Mrs I. Smith, Mrs Marks, Mr Marks, -?-, Doug Lowe, Joyce's husband, Joyce, née Hall, -?-, Desmond Phillips, Ted Roff, Mr Hopkins, Mr Lowe. Centre, with backs to the camera: Jozef Jaworski, Evelyn Dormer, Kathleen Wrighton, -?-, -?-, Mr Grey, Mrs Grey, Mrs Eva Wrighton, -?-, Evelyn Hayward, Fred Hayward, -?-, -?-, -?-, Charlie Higgs. Across the back: Mr Birch, John Hopkins, Bob West. On the right: Mr Arbetella, Mrs Eva Illing, Margaret Illing. The others are not known.

Evelyn and Jozef Jaworski (in wheelchair) watching the Meet of the Whaddon Chase Hunt arriving at the sixteenth-century Lowndes Arms, Whaddon, for the stirrup cup, *c.* 1980. The pub was named after the Selby-Lowndes family who lived at Whaddon Hall; it was previously the Haunch of Venison. The Squire, Col. W. (Billy) Selby-Lowndes, was Master of Fox Hounds from about 1929/30 and left Whaddon Hall in 1939, when it was taken over as Government offices during the Second World War.

A coach outing to Southend-on-Sea from the Lowndes Arms, Whaddon, *c.* 1950. Back row, left to right: Alec Ross, Doug Dormer, Arthur Collington, Roy Illing, Fred Wall, George Wall, Tommy Ewen, Bill Gregory, Joe Wall, -?-, Eric Toombs (landlord, in fancy hat), George Turner, -?-, Ted Robinson, Arthur Bowden, Sid Illing, Ron Radwell, Harry James, coach driver. Front row: Derek Bowden, Pat 'the Irishman', Charlie Robinson, Bill West.

Whaddon schoolchildren with their Headmistress, Miss Dorothy Meadows (from Stony Stratford), *c.* 1955. Back row, left to right: Michael Brown, Jackie Fisher, Ian Radwell, Tony Ritchie, Rosemary Adams, Ann Richie, Eileen Beckett, Miss Dorothy Meadows. Middle row (some almost hidden): Christopher Tombs, Lorna Radwell, Patsy Brown, Shirley Ross, Peter Higgs, Michael Green, Delia Pettitt, Keith Robinson, -?-, Patsy Wrighton, Sheila Gascoigne, Terry Adams, -?-, -?-. Front row: -?-, Nora Ross, Patrick Nicholson, Peter Nicholson, Avril Adams.

Hugh Willett winding the clock at St Mary's Church, Whaddon, which was installed in 1910. He regularly climbed the steep spiral staircase of the tower for thirty-four years, until shortly before his death in 1993, aged eighty-four, to rewind the two weights that activated the mechanism. Each weighed about a quarter of a ton, and to raise them fully it took about a hundred turns of the handle. Since his death the clock has been wound by electricity. As a lifelong resident of the village, he was also a chorister and bellringer.

The interior of St Giles' Church, Tattenhoe, a very small plain building (42 ft by 14 ft) showing it as it still is today, relying on candles for light: being through two fields along a farm track, it has no mains electricity. The church was rebuilt in 1540 out of the ruins of Snelshall Priory, but as the parish was small it fell into disuse. The church has been neglected through the years, but after 1842 a ceiling was put under the open tiles. Services are held between Rogation (mid-May) and Harvest Festival, when, weather permitting, the produce used to be auctioned in the churchyard.

Rarely seen today since the coming of the new town of Milton Keynes, these Shorthorn cows are obviously contented in one of the meadows of the Ebbs family, Manor Farm, Shenley Church End, *c*. 1950. Of the semi-detached houses seen in the background, the one on the right was the village post office, kept by the Goodway family, and now closed. The Barringer and Hiorns families lived in the two cottages on the right-hand bottom corner, demolished in the late 1960s. The land in the foreground is now a housing estate.

Three friends, Priscilla Daniels, Beatrice Capel and Florrie Cooper, sitting near the entrance to St Mary's Church, Shenley, when there was not a tree in sight, *c.* 1905. The thirty-six trees which now surround the church were planted by the children of the Shenley Church End Sunday school on a Sunday afternoon in 1909, watched by parents and a host of local dignitaries.

On the left is Mrs Mary Ann Perry, who kept a shop opposite Shenley post office, where children called for sweets when going to school. Standing in the centre are her son Joe and Milly Willett, whom he married. On the fence are two more of her sons: George, left, and Will, right. In the centre is Ted Willett, Milly's brother. The date is *c.* 1900.

Shenley School, 1934. Note the wickets painted on the fence for the boys who were learning to play cricket. Back row, left to right: Will Willett, Fred Daniels, Alan Weatherby, Tom Markham, Fred Hurst. Second row: Marjorie Daniels, Betty Metcalfe, Vera Willett, Dorothy Gurney, Dorothy Markham, Sybil Daniels, Margaret Powell, Gladys Wells, Monica Wells, Flossie Walduck, Peggy Bodley, Ivy Perry. Third row: May Carter, Daisy Masters, Doreen Metcalfe, Ruby Daniels, Johnny Nicholson (teacher), Erica Markham, Sylvia Perry, Elsie Toombs. Front row: Bobby Woulds, ? Essam, ? Essam, Don Foxley, Henry Hurst, Leslie Walton, Leslie Willett, George Higgs, Billy Chappell, Maurice Goodway, George Daniels, Alan Nicholson, Charlie Payne, Ted Higgs.

Reuben Hall in his cottage in London Road, Loughton, aged ninety-two, November 1975. In about 1900, when telephones were still something of a novelty, an underground cable was laid connecting London to Birmingham. It was made of solid copper and encased in cast iron. Years passed and more up-to-date cables were laid, and the plans showing the first development disappeared. Post office engineers arrived just before this photograph was taken to dig in an area which it was believed hid the early cable. They were unsuccessful, but someone sent them to Reuben, who led them to a spot a short distance from his door; sure enough they found the cable there.

Shenley Primary School, Christmas Party, 1951 or 1952. Back, left to right: Primrose Robinson, Robert Vine, -?-; John Johnson, -?-, Robert Harper, Denise Groom, Alec Johnson, Josie Smith, Hazel Weston, Maureen Hadden, -?-; Miriam Bazeley, Kenneth Oakley. Seated: -?-, -?-, -?-, -?-, -?-, Barry Davies, -?-, -?-, Philip Spires, Catherine Ebbs, Henry Owen, Keith Owen, Marlene Love, Janet Fyfe, -?-. Standing: Marilyn McGill, Mary Hiorns, Brian Massey, Christine Vine, Ann Carter, -?-, Robin Walduck, Gerald Collins, Christine Moseley, Janet Fyfe, Shirley Ann Berry, -?-, -?-, -?-, -?-; Rosalind Higgs, Karen Hasson, Ann Gascoigne, John Pattenden. Front: Rita Emmet, Tereyne Moseley, -?-, -?-; Bernard ?, Judith Ebbs, Martin Foster. On the right behind the row standing: -?-, -?-; Susanne Dolling.

A group from Shenley Church End pose for a photograph, *c.* 1900. Back row, left to right: Mr Quick (cousin of Joe Perry), Annie Willett, Joe Perry, Mrs Betsy Willett (mother of Annie and Suie). Front row: Arthur Quick (cousin of Joe Perry), Tom Smith (friend) and Suie Willett.

Charlotte Millicent (Milly) Willett, wearing a charming outfit with a parasol, is posing with her fiancé, Joseph (Joe) Perry, who is sporting his bowler hat, watchchain and cane. This *carte-de-visite* was taken by W. Alderman of Fenny Stratford.

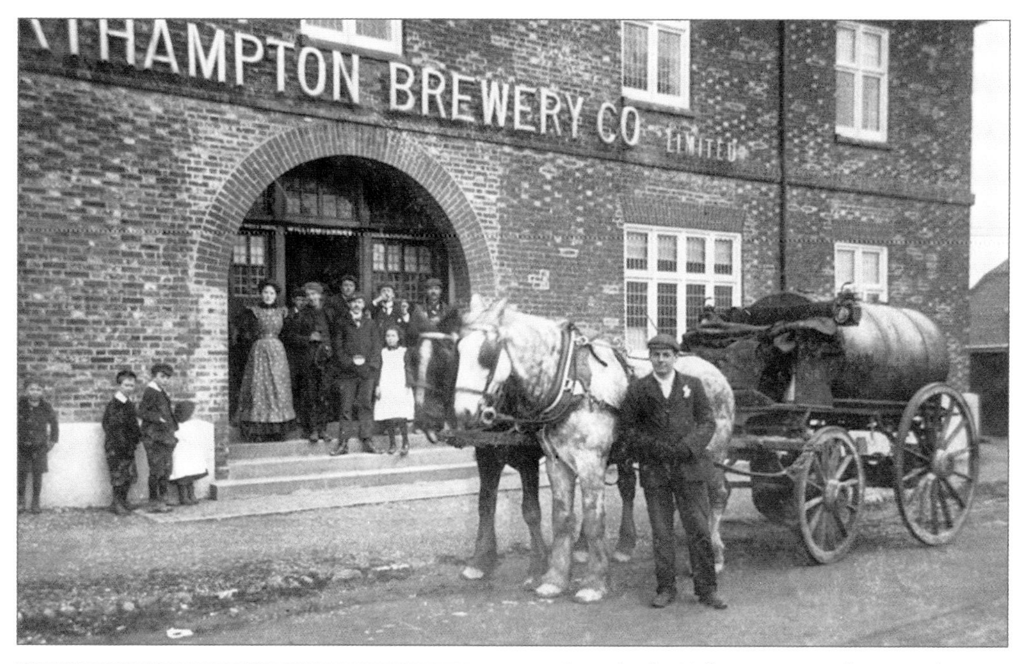

Outside the Talbot Inn, Loughton, is the paraffin cart, delivering in the village, *c.* 1910. The Talbot was first mentioned as a hostelry in 1726, but a hostelry of this name existed in 1577. It was situated on the first turnpike in England (1706), on Watling Street, from Two Mile Ash to Hockliffe.

Margaret Gurney of Rectory Farm, Loughton, out for a spin on her brother Ted's motorcycle, *c.* 1912. It has an original AA badge on the front with a Union Jack and another national flag on the handlebars. It was fashionable for girls to wear men's caps back to front with waterproof jacket and trousers.

It is difficult to picture this scene as being the main road to London – the Watling Street at Loughton. Postmarked Bletchley, 8.45 p.m., 19 February 1906, this postcard was sent by Mary Drinkwater to her sister Annie who was in service at Underbank, Elstree, Hertfordshire, to tell her that their mother had started making her aprons and would send them sometime that week. These cottages were sadly burnt when the thatch was ignited by a spark from a steam engine travelling on the London Road.

Loughton Baptist Sunday School, early 1950s. Back row, left to right: Jean Smith, Rita Sykes, -?-, Keith Owen, Pat Reading, -?-, Henry Owen. Left: ? Owen. Back centre: Judith Ebbs, Wendy Chapman, Jennifer Sykes, -?-. Next row: -?-, Susanne Dolling, Rosemary Andrews, Rosalyn Higgs, Catherine Ebbs, ? Love, Ann Carter, Shirley Berry, Graham Walker, Robin Walduck. Front left: -?-, -?-. Group right: -?-, Michael Hill, Bernard Alderman, Martin Higgs, Ian Alderman, Maureen Ebbs, Linda Walduck.

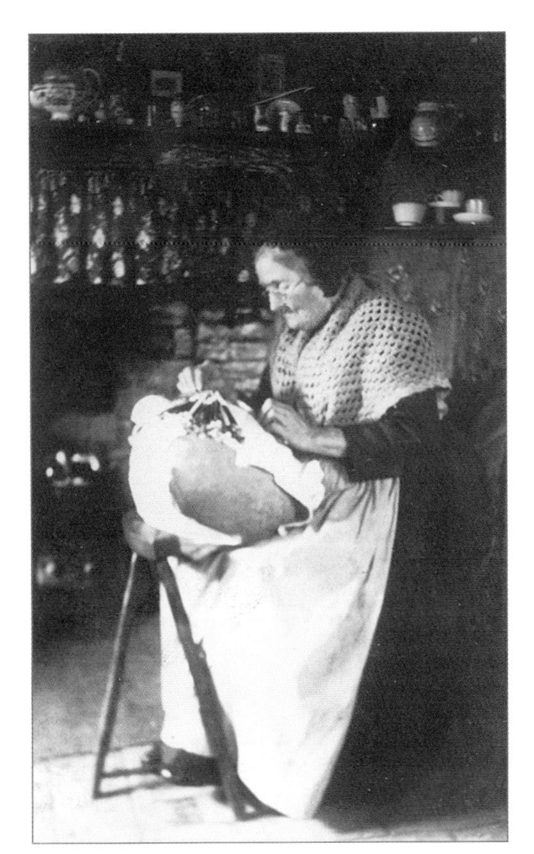

A postcard sent to 'Lizzie', *c.* 1910. It read: 'You know I dare say dear sis who this is Mrs Charlotte Gregory she is the oldest lace-maker in North Bucks just celebrated her ninetieth birthday wonderful old woman is she not.' Someone else has added: 'Charlotte Gregory aged ninety at Loughton smoked clay pipe when lace-making and could spit into the fire with great accuracy.'!

At the church of St Lawrence, Old Bradwell, Gordon Bignell (left) and Ken Beatty (right) help to install the new bell. This replaced the cracked 4th bell which originally weighed 5 cwt 0 qtrs 12 lb: it was cast by John Walgrave in 1440 and is now preserved in an aisle of the church. The first peal on the bells with the new 4th took place on 29 November 1981. The vicar was then the Revd David Bowen, who later moved to Cleveland. The bells were originally a ground-floor ring with a 40 ft draught (rope length). Following the reordering of the church interior, they are now rung from a gallery.

A view no longer to be seen, the Monks Walk, Bradwell Abbey Farm, *c.* 1900. In the seventeenth century the Longville family lived at Bradwell. In 1666 the estate was purchased by Sir Joseph Alston, who enlarged the house, restored the chapel and created a park with a fine avenue of oak trees running west from the house. These were felled during the Second World War when the land was cultivated for the war effort.

Mrs Ellen Turner (née Tue) with her daughters Mary and Olive sitting in their unusual conveyance at Turners Nurseries, Old Bradwell, *c.* 1923.

Old Bradwell School, *c.* 1925. It opened in the late 1880s and closed in 1952. Back row, left to right: ? Young, Cyril Whitlock, Alan King, Douglas Gardner, Winnie Geary, Peter Briggs, Alf Goodger, Tim Levitt. Second row: Norman Robinson, Raymond Briggs, -?-, Nora Grey, Hughie Simpson, Olive Turner, -?-, Steve Kingston. Third row: Ken Bird, Lily Whitlock, Sylvia Barnes, Eva Daniels, Tony Townsend, -?-, V. Webb, Edna Foulkes, -?-, -?-. Front row Douglas Hendricks, -?-, Norman Chapman, -?-, Harry Young, Edwin Tuckey, Arthur Brown, George Grey.

Samuel Partridge in his back garden, High Street, Haversham, *c.* 1950. He is sawing up his firewood with a large circular saw. Note the old lineprops, one on the left and one with washing on the line, on the right. A woodman would come round the streets and backways to houses, selling these, and also pea sticks and faggots cut out of the woods. To attract customers' attention they used to call 'Line-props Line-props!'

Dorothy Pearce, a Land Army girl during the Second World War, carrying milking machines at Thomas Paton's Hill Farm, Haversham.

This herd of Ayrshires is in the milking parlour of Thomas Paton's farm. Arriving from Scotland on 25 November 1955, he hired a train and brought his herd and equipment with him. He eventually ceased milking and sold his Ayrshire herd.

On Wednesday 18 October 1939 seven hours of torrential rain caused large-scale flooding in Northamptonshire, Buckinghamshire, Bedfordshire and Leicestershire. The picture shows the new 30 ft long bridge over the River Ouse on the Wolverton–Hanslope–Northampton road at Haversham, a mile from Wolverton LMS railway station, which gave way at about noon. Claude Meakins of Haversham was the last person to crawl over the parapet before it too disappeared into the swirling waters.

Robert Adams, with his wife and family, who in 1857 purchased Bradwell Windmill with the intention of setting his ward, John Abbott, up in business. John was not interested, however, so Robert's son, also Robert Adams, moved to Mill Cottage and ran the business. In 1871 John Abbott sold his share of Boughton Green Fair, and Robert Adams then moved to Carr's Mill, Haversham. Shortly afterwards the mill ceased working, Samuel Holman erected the smock mill in 1805 in a 9 acre field called the Yawls at Bradwell. Now a Grade II listed building, it is open to the public, particularly on May Day.

The wedding of Arthur Child to Beatrice Barnes, *c.* 1908. Their familes lived next door to one another in Queen Anne Street, New Bradwell. The Child family lived in Oak Cottage. Back row, left to right: Nellie Abbey, Mrs and Mr Brookes (cousin of bride), Lilley Child (sister of bridegroom), Harry Child (brother of bridegroom), Gertrude Barnes and Harry Barnes (married to each other; Harry was brother of the bride), Mabel Bull (bride's sister), John Bull and baby Tom Bull. Second row: Ada Child (married Frank Stanton), Daisy Child, Elizabeth Bradshaw (bridegroom's grandmother from Lidlington, Bedfordshire. Her husband was a blacksmith who made all the gutterings, etc. for the railway houses in New Bradwell), Caroline Child (née Bradshaw, mother of bridegroom), ? Masters (nephew of bride), Joseph Child (bridegroom's father), Mrs Barnes and Mr Barnes (bride's mother and father), Mrs Barnes and Mr Barnes (brother of bride and his wife). Third row: Frank Stanton, Mary Masters (niece of bride), Gertrude Child (sister of the bridegroom), Arthur Child (bridegroom), Beatrice Barnes (bride), Lily (niece of the bride), Elsie Child (sister of bridegroom), Adelaide Child (sister of bridegroom), Leonard Dixon (who married Adelaide Child the following year). Front row: -?- (nephew of the bride), Bertha Child (bridegroom's sister).

Bradwell United Silver Prize Band formed in 1901, and has an unbroken tradition of almost 100 years. On 6 June 1930 their President, Dr Charles Miles, died and left the band a legacy of £100 with which they decided to buy new uniforms. They made a parade of the town one Sunday morning looking smart in uniforms of dark brown with green and gold facings, and made a collection en route through the streets to which people liberally responded. This photograph shows the new uniforms, 1932. Back row, left to right: W. Kightley, C. Bissell, W. Campbell, H. Walters, R. Bennett, B. Breedon, S. Eldred. Middle row: E. Campbell, G. Meakins, T. Cox, W. Frost, R. Smart, S. Saunders, F. Walton, A. Campbell. Front row: E. Meakins, T. Kightley, C. Mynard, M. Pepper, J.E. Johnson (Bandmaster), P. Hardwick (Assistant-Bandmaster) W. Walters (Secretary), W. Mallard, C. Norwood.

Bradwell bandsman Bill Frost's young son Ronald holding his father's baritone, *c*. 1946, and hoping one day he will join him in the Bradwell United Silver Prize Band.

Dr Charles Henry Miles of The Laurels, New Bradwell, 1900s. Born on 8 January 1859, Dr Miles was grandson of Martin Miles of Tyrrels Manor, Stoke Hammond, Buckinghamshire, and Lord of the Manor. He was a member of the Royal Bucks Hussars for seven years and was a prize shot and prize swordsman between 1881 and 1883. Charles is seen here with his wife Alice Harriett, daughter of the Revd Charles Purcell Cotter MA, Vicar of Stantonbury for thirty-three years. The couple are enjoying a drive in his carriage, which he used when visiting his patients.

Nineteen young ladies competed to become Bradwell Carnival Queen in 1948. Molly Adams was chosen to be the first Miss Bradwell since the Second World War, and is seen here with her attendants. Standing left to right: Amy Wood, Vera Clarke, Daphne McLeod, -?-. Seated: Dorothy Crawford, Molly Adams, Doreen Clarke (who carried the crown), Kathleen Lane.

New Bradwell Junior School, 1951. Back row, left to right: Ivor Price, Arthur Adkins, Gordon Noble, Roy Reynolds, Christopher Atkins, Michael Thomas, Robert Ogden, Alan Arthur, Terry Corkett, Barry Casebrook, Roger Westley. Second row: Robert Gentles, Margaret Bird, Dilys Drinkwater, Yvonne Jerham, Marion Huckle, Georgina Nash, Ann Morley, Margaret Packer, Carol Heap, Sheila Alderman, Linda Jelly, Tony Wootton. Third row: Malcolm Sambrook, Alan Johnson, Maureen Smart, Wendy Smith, Ken Healey (teacher), Diane Faithfull, Linda Lankaster, Alan Capel, Ken Challinor. Front row: Roy Pateman, Les Marshall, Cecily Durham, Stanley Simms, Ivan Lantsberry.

Headmaster and teachers, New Bradwell Junior School, 1957. Back row, left to right: Mrs A. Baines, Ken Speaks, Miss J. Clarke, R. Stevens, Mrs Haydn, Harvey Hayward, Mrs Clarke. Front row: Mrs McNeil, Mr B.J. Salmons (Headmaster), Mrs Williams.

The New Inn darts team, New Bradwell, *c.* 1959/60. Back row, left to right: Vic Ewins, Tommy Emerton, Mick Emerton, George Odell, Ron Frost, Arthur Godfrey. Front row: Sam Tuckey, Tom Howard, Bill Taft, Geoff Odell.

One could buy winkles in a pint pot before the First World War from Mr and Mrs Busby on Sunday afternoons, on what became known as Busby's Corner at the foot of the Canal Hill, New Bradwell. They also sold cockles, mussels, oysters and whelks. The cats obviously knew where to come for titbits! When people committed suicide, or drank too much in the Black Horse or the New Inn and fell into the canal, the police engaged Bert Busby to get the body out and transport it on his cart.

The presentation of a seat to Wolverton Urban District Council by Wolverton Labour Party, in appreciation of the excellent work done for the town by Councillor W.H. Lee, early 1960s. The photograph was taken on the Square, where the seat remained for many years. The lady on the extreme left should not have been in the photo; Miss Nock just walked across the Square and joined the group! Back row, left to right: Miss Nock, Miss Aileen Button, Reg Westley, Neville Crook, Jim Dewick, Bill Hilton, Donald Morgan, -?-, Charles Russell, ? Goodridge, Terry Crook, Brian Barnard (Labour Party agent). Middle row: Mrs Eva Faulkner, Mrs Ernie Richardson. Front row: Alec Lambert, Frank Atter, Mrs W.H. Lee, Dr John Love (Chairman of WUDC), Mr Billy Lee (the gentleman whose work was commemorated by the gift of the seat), the niece of Mr and Mrs Lee.

Wolverton Conservative Association ladies outing, mid-1940s. Back row, left to right: Mrs Ernie Brocklehurst, Mrs Bill Jakeman, Mrs Bradbury, Mrs Sid Smith, Mrs Arthur Held, Mrs Bill Barley, Mrs Bill Eady, Mrs Walter Beasley, Mrs Long, Mrs Phillips, Mrs Burrows, -?-. Middle row: Mrs Newman, Mrs Frank Chapman, Mrs Mary Tompkins, Mrs Albert Dearn, Mrs Allan, Mrs Tandy, Mrs Bill Tompkins, Mrs W.H. Sykes, Mrs Newmans, Mrs Hussey. Front row: Mrs Bill Glave, Mrs Cartmail, Mrs Fleet, Mrs William Coleman, Mrs Walters, Mrs Wilson, Mrs Rogers, Mrs Joe Smart, Mrs A.H. Holland.

Bob Garratt, in light jacket, of Hanslope held a small select dinner party at the Craufurd Arms, Wolverton on 28 August 1970. To get an invitation you had to remember pre-First World War training camps with the 1st Bucks Battalion, and the four-day march from Dunstable to Chelmsford. Mr Garratt cut the special cake made for the occasion by his neighbour Mrs Muriel Ditum. In all there were 14 former members, whose ages totalled 1,074 years. Between them they shared nearly a hundred medals, including two DCMs, two MMs and an MSM. Back row, left to right: Harry Syratt (76), Bert Brawn (80), Sid Southam (79), Arthur Willis (74), Jim Read (77), Joe Lovesy (77), Felix Johnson (76), Charlie Foulkes (76). Front row: Billy Batterson (76), Jack Biggs (74), Tommy Hopcroft (77), Herbert Waine (79). Bob Hart (76) was not present when the picture was taken.

What a thrill to be in Wolverton Carnival on no. 2 float for the Conservative Club, which used a railway dray, *c.* 1933. Their Royal Scot train model, engine no. 6110, can be seen in the centre and would have won if raised higher. Eileen Jakeman remembers wearing a Scottish tartan outfit on a very hot day! Two others represented a rose and a thistle. Left to right: Jean Robinson, Betty Pearce, Eileen Brickwood, Ted Ellery, Joyce Harrison, Mary, Eileen and Lena Jakeman.

There were ten boys in the first patrol of 1st Wolverton Scouts, all pictured here at their first camp in Deanshanger at Easter, March 1908. The scoutmaster Charlie Aplin took the photograph – he was a keen photographer.

The seven surviving members of the first patrol of 1st Wolverton Boy Scouts (troop formed 23 February 1908, the first in Buckinghamshire) at the fiftieth anniversary, 1958. Left to right: B. Throsby, J. Scragg, Ernie Causer, Bill Eady, Harry Causer, H. Cadwallader, J. George. Others were W. (Billy) Henson, H. Nicholls and F. Fincher. Scoutmaster Charlie Aplin was killed during the First World War, in 1916.

Mind that ear! Keith Webb one of the 1st Wolverton Scouts, all lathered up and shaving at camp with a cut-throat razor. Note the strop on the tentpole, a leather for sharpening the razor.

Five Wolf Cubs dressed as the Dionne Quintuplets (who had been born two years previously in Callander, Ontario, Canada), Marie, Cecilie, Emilie, Yvonne and Annette. They were the 1st Wolverton Wolf Cubs entry in the Northampton Hospital Gala Day, Saturday 25 July 1936. The bumper pram was made from scratch by the Scouts and won first prize, 10*s*. Fred Frisby, King's Scout, pushed the pram all round the streets of Wolverton accompanied by nurses, doctor, milkman and 'Mr and Mrs Dionne'. The man standing at the side in Scout uniform is Wally Clarke.

HRH the Duke of Connaught's Challenge Shield Competition, 1956. An international rifle shooting competition started in 1911, this was open to a team of four scouts from any group in Great Britain and overseas that was registered at Imperial HQ. At only their second attempt 1st Wolverton Boy Scout troop won the shield, obtaining 772 points out of a possible 800. In addition to the team award, one of the team, Gordon Hill, won the silver medal presented by the National Small Bore Rifle Association for the highest individual score, gaining 99 out of a possible 100. Left to right: Mr Tatham (Secretary of Wolverton Rifle Club), Graham Wright, Gordon Hill, Richard Ratcliffe, ASL Tom Smith (trainer). P. Vousden was absent.

Jack Hurry's retirement presentation at McCorquodale Envelope Works, Wolverton, *c.* 1973. Left to right: Vera Scragg, Cecil Lloyd, Janet Grey, Dennis Rowledge, George Boddington, Violet Harris, Joe Berridge, Jack Hurry (Works Supervisor), May Williamson, Bet Ellis, Kathleen Atkinson, Deborah Brown, Bob Bull (Envelope Works Manager), John Cooper (Departmental Supervisor, Envelope Room), Hazel Richardson, Doreen Stewart, Gwen Ridgeway, Joan Eglesfield, Margaret Swannell.

Wolverton District Guides (1st Wolverton, 1st Stony Stratford and Castlethorpe and Hanslope) off to camp at Lamberhurst, Kent, 1968. In the coach: Pat Earp, Maureen Healey, with, below them, Margaret and Sue Bird. Back row, left to right: Beverley Ward (Hanslope), Lesley O'Connor (Hanslope), Barbara Yates, Cathryn Stock, Susan Fitch, Vanessa Millward, -?-, Laura Youlton, Yvonne Swannell, Susan Holt, Julie Swann, Kay Murgatroyd, Barbara Mead, Dawn French, Felicity Light, and Guiders Edith Stevens, Rene Healey, Jean Bird, Joyce Markham. Kneeling at front: ? Saunders, Susan Yates, Cheryl Ward (Hanslope), Susan King, Sheila Bavington, Rosemary Marks (Hanslope), Helen ?, Tina Thorn, Cheryl Earp, -?-, Heather Wright, Christine Eales, Beverley ?, Elaine Russell, Deborah French.

Trying out the new postage stamp machines at the opening of Wolverton post office in Church Street. The date is carved in stonework at the entrance, 'George VI 1937'.

Some members of Wolverton BR and Town Band at their practice in the British Rail Dining Hall on Sunday 5 October 1969, before coming third in the National Brass Band Championships. In 1923 the band won third prize in the third section at the Crystal Palace when young Doug Dytham was playing. Now, forty-six years later, he is once more among the bandsmen. Doug formed his own band, 'The Rhythm Aces', before the Second World War, and disbanded it some fifty-seven years later in 1980. Sid was also a popular entertainer, as he played the saw and did impressive rendition of 'The Post-Horn Gallop' on a post-horn. Back row, left to right: Ted Briggs, Robert Wills, Nick Dytham, Ian Stewart, Fred Atkins. Front row: Sid Dytham, Douglas Dytham, Jonathan Whetstone, Doug Horton, Sam Horton, Robert Pickup.

Wolverton Congregational Juniors FC, 1936/7. They were winners of the Buckingham Senior Hospital Cup, the Wolverton Hospital Cup, and runners-up for the Bletchley Hospital Cup. Back row, left to right: S. Willett (committee), G. Glave, E. Bull, B. Wyatt, J. Jones (committee). Middle row: B. Henson (linesman), S. Tuckey (Trainer), G. Frost, V. Gee, J. Cooper (Capt.), L. Gee (Hon. Secretary), H. Clarke, H. Willett (Chairman). Front row: V. Stevens, T. Clarke, H. Franklin, F. Miles, R. Jones.

Wolverton Town Football Club 2nd XI, 1953/4. Back row, left to right: Jimmy Briscoe (Coach: he also trained the Cobblers, Northampton), S. Nichols, D. Drage, Peter Hill, Peter Cosford, R. Sheffield, Keith Webb, W. Haynes (Trainer). Front row: W. Kightley, Alec Levitt, Jack Goldsmith, William (Bill) Castle, D. Stones.

Wolverton Infants School, Class I, 1932. Back row, left to right: Peter Battison, John Hemming, Joan Hopcroft, Marjorie Welford, Ruby Tysoe, Una James, Robert Percival, Leslie Gear, William Townsend, Stanley King, Beryl Garrett, Muriel Townsend. Middle row: Hilda Howlett, Clifford Hillyard, Stanley Hillyard, Eric Rice, Ronald Emery, Kenneth Speaks, Stanley Jones, Stanley Taylor, Arthur Webber, Walter Coleman, Joyce Goodridge, David Lloyd, Derek Parker. Front row: Dorothy Spong, Arthur Spong, Vera Underwood, Betty Underwood, Vera Holloway, Ray Holloway, Eileen Brickwood, Alan Leach, Doris Shakeshaft, James Shakeshaft, Joan Bush, Norman Spires.

The Tempest, performed by Wolverton Girls Council School, 1935 or 1936. Group top left, left to right: Phyllis Coles, Betty Pearce, Sonia Cunniffe. Back row: Margaret Seamarks, Irene Terry, Janet Gould, Joan Stimpson, Gwen Cooper, Christine Percival, Joan Wood, Gladys Squire, Phyllis Pack, Joan Bubb, Ivy Johnson, ? Brewer, Maud Smith, ? Brewer. Centre row, kneeling: -?-, Dorothy Snowdon, Joy Jerham, Gladys Smith, -?-, Joan Stubbs, Mary Jakeman, Eileen Brickwood. Front row, sitting: Muriel Townsend, Kathleen Wilks, -?-, Marjorie Tissington, Kathleen Dunn, Doreen Mackay, Gwen Brocklehurst, Kathleen Little.

Wolverton County Junior School 1st XI, 1970/1. The team was unbeaten in this season and won the local school cup. The teacher was Mr K. Riddy. Back row, left to right: Ian Stewart, Perry Essam, Ronnie Humphries, Mark Walters, Mark Bennett, Philip Held. Middle row: Richard Massey, Tony Martin, Ian Slaymaker, John Parker, Stephen E. Hayfield. Front row: Gary Lyons, Michael Chappell.

Retiring presentations at Bushfield School, Wolverton, to Mr R. Garner (Headmaster) and Miss N. Bird (a teacher there for many years), July 1974. Back row, left to right: Mr B. Craddock, Mrs Ivy French, Miss Susan Harris, Elaine Hetherington, -?-, Mrs Janice Hooton, Mr John Smith, Mr Alan Bateman. Middle row: Mrs Heather Georgeson, Miss Lyn Barnett, Mrs Mary Boughton, Miss Joan Pennington, Mrs Rene Healey, Mrs Muriel Cosford, Mr Sharman, Mrs Lyn Thomas, Mr Ken Speaks. At the front: Miss Nellie Bird, Mr Ronald Garner. One teacher is absent, so is probably a supply teacher.

Thomas Cadwallader and his family outside their home, the Institute House, 5 Church Street, Wolverton, *c.* 1902. He was Librarian to the Science and Art Institute, which changed its name to Wolverton Technical College when he became Secretary. Back row, left to right: Elsie, Aubrey, Madge, William Thomas, Florence. Front row: Tom Cadwallader, Harold, Rose (née Storey, Tom's wife).

Wolverton Technical College: the last sports day for 6c, who left school in July 1950. Back row, left to right: Margaret Geen, Ruth Claydon, Rosemary Stone, Mary Herbert, Miss Ethel Smith, Miss Mary Thompson, Hazel Mettam, Julia Cafe, Barbara Downing, Peggy Ratcliffe. Middle row: Kathleen Wrighton, Jeane Line, Yvonne Thatcher, Daphne Davies, Beryl Chambers, Faith Beckett, Enid Wilson. Front row: Diane Eglesfield, Nina Eales, Joyce Parker, Sylvia Harding, June Hinton. In the distance on the left: Shirley Ellis.

J.C. Barnes' lithograph of the railway embankment in course of construction to carry the London & Birmingham Railway across the Wolverton valley, June 1837. Wolverton had two mills, one at each end, mentioned in the Domesday Book. On the left can be seen the one on the eastern side, Mead Mill, which was still mentioned in the 1851 census. Woods Mill or Wolverton West Mill was, in 1887, a water-driven mill run by F. Wood. It ceased working some years ago, and while the exterior remains almost unaltered the interior is now apartments.

A meeting outside the Wolverton railway works, calling for volunteers to serve in the First World War, September 1914. The man with a beard in the centre is Edward Newman, who had fought in the South African War, and was Quarter Master Sergeant, QMS Queen's Hussars, serving for twenty years. The man with his cap sideways, fifth from right, is his son, John Henry Newman, who promptly volunteered to serve during the First World War. The works chimney, seen in the distance, was a well-known landmark until demolished a few years ago.

Maurice Wise of Old Stratford working in Wolverton Railway Works, 1950s. He was a marker out in the sawmill. This was a skilled job; markers never did any cutting.

The 'girls' (shorthand typists and clerks) in the Production Planning Office of Wolverton Carriage & Wagon Works, 4 January 1956. Note the decorated window sill, one of about six on which seasonal scenes were arranged each Christmas. Group on left: back row, left to right: Edith Shelton, Joan Nunn, Phyllis Keech, Cis Claridge (née Henson). Front row: Audrey Cooper (née Waine), Pat Stanton, Glenys Taylor. Group on right, back row: Mabel Overhead, Mavis Hawtin (née Peer). Front row: Nellie Campion, Joy Rogoff, Mrs Bignell.

Joiners and Smiths, winners of the LMS inter-shop competition, Wolverton Works, 1931. Back row, left to right: R.J. Durdin, L.C.W. Wood, G.E. Hedge, G. Foddy, H.A. Cook, A. Walton, H. Riley. Front row: T.W. Impey, W. Childs, A. Chilton, H.T. Curtis (Vice-Capt.). H. Smith (Capt.), E.F. Waine, F. Bull.

The coaches of the Royal Train are housed at Wolverton Railway Works. This is the Wolverton Royal Train crew who took the Prince of Wales to Caernarvon for his Investiture, July 1969. Back row, left to right: Ernie Henson, Gerald Kingston, Dick Henson, Tom Carter, Eric Barnes, Arthur Cowley. Front row: Jack Preston, Arthur Harrup, Stan Butler (Royal Train Supervisor), George Stevens. Stan Butler, in his twenty-seven years on the train, twenty-five as Foreman/Supervisor, received the Queen's Silver Jubilee Medal in 1977 for his work in keeping the royal train in top travelling order, and on 21 February 1989 went to Buckingham Palace to collect his Royal Victoria Medal, awarded exclusively by the Queen.

1st Wolverton Brownie pack, *c.* 1946. Back row, left to right: Enid Thomas, Yvonne Wills, ? Cockerill, Pat Temple, Shirley Williams, Pauline Durdin, Ruth Walker, Molly Dewick, Valerie Birchenough, Sheila Pell, -?-. Second row: Phyllis Mackerness, Christine Stubbs, Rosemary Jerham, Anthea West, Janet Bull, -?-, Janet Griffiths. Third row: Joan Callow, Jean Atterbury, Ann Valentine, Jean Davies, Ethel Howarth, Mary Jakeman, Marjorie Hart, Pamela Elliott, Jean Henson, Joy Johnson, Betty Dewick. Front row: Jean Bassingthwaite, Ann Howarth, Jennifer Swann, Alma Berridge.

From the mid-1880s the Railway Works has always possessed a first class ambulance team. This is Wolverton 'A' Ambulance Team, 1938, winners of the LMS Railway English and International championships. Back row, left to right: F.H. Clarke (Hon. Asst Secretary), W.J. Barby (Hon. Secretary), J.O. Ibell (Hon. Dist. Secretary), Dr D.W.A. Bull JP, A.G. Felts (Chairman), B.J. Willett (Instructor). Front row: D.G.N. Goodridge (reserve), L.H. Billingham, S.W. Andrews, S.A. Webber (Captain), W.J. Richardson, H.J. Green, B. Stevens (reserve).

Wolverton St John's Nursing Division, *c.* 1944. The nurses' married names are in brackets. Back row, left to right: Ivy Jolley (Mrs Watson), Betty Goodway (Mrs Glave), Elsie Spiers, Beattie Hall, Jean Nelson (Mrs Pearson), Betty Lloyd (Mrs Morton), Rose Simons, -?- (Mrs Tootill), Betty Cook (Mrs Wise). Middle row: Kitty Snowdon (Mrs Tite), Sylvia ? (Mrs Eales), Barbara Harding (Mrs Jarvis), -?- (Mrs Hilliard), ? (Mrs Earl), Dorothy Snowdon (Mrs Iles), Elsie Hughes (Mrs Shean), Eileen Andrews, Phyllis Pack (Mrs Meakins), Mary Jakeman (Mrs Webb). Front row: May Saunders (Mrs Garwood), -?- (Mrs Sellick), Marjorie Dunleavy, -?- (Mrs Cook), Mrs Peters (wife of Railway Works Superintendent), Nurse Stafford (Mrs Nutt), Margaret Thompson, Lily Cook (Mrs Wood).

Sitting proudly on his motorcycle is Bertie Henson, who was one of the first owners of a motorbike in Wolverton, *c.* 1913.

The Revd G. Mower conducting the last morning service in Wolverton Congregational Church, 5 April 1970. Thi church was built in 1878, and the new church was built on the same site at the corner of Radcliffe Street anc Aylesbury Street, on the south-eastern corner of the Square. A large shop occupied the ground floor for a perioc while the church, now United Reformed, is on the first floor. The photograph includes Mrs Procter, Mr anc Mrs Tompkins, Margaret Tompkins, Ernest Slater, Myra Slater, Mr and Mrs Allen, Mrs Mower, Margare Thompson, Irene Healey, Jean Pickup, Mrs Asprey, Mrs Phyllis Light, Betty Brandom, Philip Atkins, Felicity Light Julie West, Linda Hill, Julie Swann, Linda Maunders, Deborah French, Sheila Mackintosh, Mrs Joan French, Dian West and Susan Herring.

Winsor & Glave: Harry Winsor in his DIY Store, 43 Jersey Road, Wolverton. The original business was purchased by brothers William J. and John E.S. Winsor and John B. Glave on 12 July 1919. Work included making chassis for Co-operative vans, furniture for Co-op stores, and alterations to business premises. A Model T Ford belonging to Mr J.H. Bates was used during the day, then swept clean, the vehicle body housed in the garage roof was lowered, seats installed, and then Mr Bates conveyed passengers to nearby towns in the evening. William Winsor died in 1965. His son Harry took over and extended the firm, which eventually had three departments – Furniture, Building and DIY. Harry sold the business and retired in about 1985.

The 'miniature Woolworths' at Ratcliffe Street corner, Wolverton, belonged to Mr Hutchinson. Here in about 1910, we see Father Christmas calling at Mr Hutchinson's: 'Tell all the Boys and Girls that I am leaving my BEST TOYS at your shop and anything they see in your windows, and want, if they will tell their Fathers and Mothers, Father Xmas will put it in their stockings.' Mr Hutchinson was an uncle of George Hill, who started at the shop in about 1901 as a lather boy aged ten, after school. He later lived in Sherington – an apiarist, farmer, a member of Sherington British Legion and a woodwork instructor for the Railway Works apprentices.

Jean and Barbara Turney and their friend Helen Campbell on Jean's donkey Bill at Warren Farm, Old Wolverton, early 1930s. Bill was quite a character: he liked walking on grass but not on gravel and would throw one off in a trice! He often kicked up his heels and chucked his riders off. They sometimes put him in front of the lawnmower. He came to an untimely end, when he was struck by lightning and killed while sheltering under a tree in his field during a thunderstorm.

A nice aerial view of Warren Farm, Old Wolverton, before the coming of the new town of Milton Keynes, 1960s. Towards the back of the photograph, on the right, is the Old Farmhouse, built in the eighteenth century and later called The Cottage. It has three storeys at the back and two storeys at the garden front. Mr Barrett was the last farmer here. In the foreground is the new Warren Farmhouse, built in 1899 to replace the old one, facing Stony Stratford. The Turney family were the last tenant farmers of the Radcliffe Trustees, who sold to the Milton Keynes Development Corporation. All is now offices except one barn.

Mr Richard (Dick) Maycock with his herd of cows at milking time, *c.* 1964. This was once a common sight at Old Wolverton Mill, but the land is no longer farmed. Mr Maycock, born in 1894, died at the great age of 101. He had two sons, both farmers, Michael in Cosgrove and Richard, who recently moved to Whitchurch.

Having completed our circular tour, we arrive back in Stony Stratford on the tram. Its top speed was around 14 mph, and Harry Cooper records on the back of this postcard that this photograph was taken on a Saturday dinnertime at 12.15 p.m., when he was thirteen years old in 1907.

The last steam tram ran in May 1926 at the commencement of the General Strike. Here men are taking up the tram lines in Wolverton Road, Stony Stratford, in 1934. John Thomas Shean is on the right.

ACKNOWLEDGEMENTS

I would firstly like to thank my husband, Jim, for his great co-operation and forbearance during the eighteen months it has taken me to collect these photographs and to visit the many people who have named faces in the group photographs.

I am indebted to my friend Joy Brunt for giving time to write the Introduction during her many engagements as Mayor of Swindon.

I much appreciated access to various collections and wish to thank Mary Robinson – Ann Burman Collection, Richard Odell – Ron Odell Collection, Sue Morley – Joan Brockway Collection, Ron Unwin – Wolverton & District Archaeological & Historical Society Slide Collection, and Charmian Woodfield for the gift of negatives from F.G. Bavey, Photographer Collection.

Some photographs could not have been reproduced unless enhanced by Ray Rowlson Photographers, and Roger Welling who restored and copied old photographs.

Also, my thanks to Michelle Thomas of Stony Stratford Library for her help with research and to other people who provided historical information. Thanks are due to those listed below who kindly loaned their personal photographs, without which this book would not have been possible: Carolyn Adams, Robert Adams, Robert Ayers, Bill Barby, Brian Barnes, Winifred Bates, Ray Bellchambers, Barbara and Anthony Bellham, Margaret Bignell, Wendy Bluck, Les Braggins, Peter Brazell, Peter Briggs, Stan Butler, Elizabeth Chapman, Sid and Edie Chapman, Michael Chappell, Dorothy and Denis Chipperfield, Ruth Clare, John Cooper, Enid and Bill Coxhill, Philip Cross, Beryl Croxford, Bill Daniell, Eric and Gerald Ditum, Joan Dolling, Rosemary and Nick Dytham, Dorothy Ebbs, Cyril Eden, Rose Elliott, Owen Fenson, Ruby Fisher, Ann Foddy, Julie Franklin, Gerald Freestone, Ronald and William Frost, Eva Gascoigne, Wendy Gladwyn, Gerald Godfrey, Katie Green, Olive and Arthur Harrison, John Haseldine, Irene Healey, Doll Hebson, Mary Henson, Mitch Hicks, Joyce Hockings, Evelyn Holbrook, Irene Holland, Pam Holman, Betty and Doug Holloway, Edith Holyhead, Lena Jakeman, Evelyn Jaworska, Molly Kightley, Margaret Ladd, Olive Lambert, Wendy and Richard Maycock, Stanley Meadows, Ann Mills, Kay Moroney, Jack Newman, Dora Nicholls, Ralph Nichols, Marjorie Norman, Fr Ross Northing, Josie Oakley, Rosalie Osborne, Evelyn Pateman, Beryl Perkins, Ian Phelps, Susan Radband, Mary Ramsay, Pam Reynolds, Mary Rogers, Stan Russell, Mary Saggers, Enid and Ray Scarsbrook, Syd Sharp, Winnie Shean, Phyllis Shirley, Diana Smith, Ken Speaks, Ann Stainsby, Sue Starr, Jean and John Starsmore, Dorothy Stevens, Gweneth Stock, Margaret Summers, Betty Sutton, Linda Tipple, Kitty Tite, Jean Tweedale, Daphne Tween, Hilda Unwin, Sue Vinden, Joan and Frank Walker, Hazel Wallis, Evelyn Webb, Mary Webb, Bill West, Bob West, Ann Westley, Reg Westley, Harry Winsor, David Wise, Charmian Woodfield, Alex Wootton, Michael Wootton, Helen Zach.

I hope I have not omitted anyone, but if so I trust you will accept my sincere apologies.